Best Knickers Always

🖐 ⬜ ✖ ✖ ;-)

50 LESSONS FOR MIDLIFE

Rebecca Perkins

An Orion paperback

First published in Great Britain in 2014
by Orion Books Ltd,
Orion House, 5 Upper St Martin's Lane,
London WC2H 9EA

An Hachette UK company

1 3 5 7 9 10 8 6 4 2

A CIP catalogue record for this book
is available from the British Library.

ISBN (Paperback) 978 1 4091 5015 2
ISBN (Ebook) 978 1 4091 5016 9

Printed and bound in Great Britain by Clays Ltd, St Ives plc

The Orion Publishing Group's policy is to use papers
that are natural, renewable and recyclable products and
made from wood grown in sustainable forests. The logging
and manufacturing processes are expected to conform to
the environmental regulations of the country of origin.

www.orionbooks.co.uk

For Oliver, Beatrice and Daniel.

You are the wind beneath my wings; you teach me
to love and to trust, to be courageous and resilient.
I am blessed.
I love you with all my heart.

Acknowledgements

This book would not have been possible without the love, support and encouragement of my 3 a.m. tribe, those women and men who just wouldn't take my procrastinations any longer. I give thanks to you all, especially Bridget Robinson, Dave Graceson, Stephen Cotterell, Sarah Maliphant, Maria Farmery, Maureen Hannan and Rachel Alexander.

I acknowledge, thank and am overwhelmingly grateful to Kate Mills my editor and publisher for hearing my voice. This is just the beginning.

Book writing is a collaboration, always. I have innumerable people to thank, many of whom I have assured anonymity. I love you. My children for their unconditional love and patience, you are my greatest achievements, I'm so proud to hear you call me Mama. To all those I bombarded on Facebook and Twitter for thoughts and support, thank you for all the fun we've had. I love Social Media. And, finally, Jane Anderson for the text that has taken on a life of its own . . . Best Knickers Always, girl!

With love and gratitude always.

'*And the time came when the risk to remain tight in the bud was more painful than the risk it took to blossom.*'

Anaïs Nin

About Me

I am an ordinary woman. I'm a daughter, a sister, a
mother and I've been a wife. I'm not perfect. I've been
through a painful divorce after a twenty-one-year marriage
and am now thriving. I've suffered years of depression and
come through it, stronger and more at ease with who I am.
I've dealt with serious illness within the family and we've

survived. I have faced (and still face) my own demons of low self-esteem, my fears of not being good enough and battles with my own self-worth. Do I wish I'd been dealt a different hand of cards in this life? Absolutely not. I would not change a single thing. Even those days, those very dark days when my daughter's anorexia was an almost unbearable weight around my neck, when I could barely get out of bed because of my depression, even during the most difficult days of my divorce, I would not change a day. I am the woman I am today because of the richness of my life experiences.

I write about the ordinary stuff of women's lives. I hope to inspire you, by example, to become happier, freer within yourself, more successful, wiser, more enlightened and empowered. I choose to write truthfully, oftentimes for me that means painfully. I choose to open my heart in my writing and that causes me to revisit the places I've been deeply unhappy. I wanted to do this to show you that it is possible to come out the other side of hardship and pain. To be happier, more grateful and stronger than you might think possible right now. I am, however, no fool. I know that there will be tough times ahead too, but I will face them with acceptance and understanding, knowing that they too will pass.

I write as a woman who has recently celebrated her fiftieth birthday. And I do mean celebrated rather than turned fifty as this is what I feel about being fifty. For me it is a celebration. I spoke with my twenty-year-old daughter recently who has so much of her life ahead of her, university education to complete, career to choose, adventures to have and memories to create; she is, at twenty, setting out on her journey of womanhood. I am grateful for my fifty years, I would not wish to be twenty again. I love my wisdom, I love my self-confidence, I love that I will no longer suffer fools, I love that women of our generation have choices. We can make choices for our lives that our mothers, aunts and grandmothers could not make. We can choose to set up our own business, we can choose to look younger, we can choose to end an unhappy marriage, we can choose to go back to college, we can choose to travel alone. These are all real choices. We must, however, have the belief that we have the free will to make those choices.

Introduction

Life isn't always (and let's be honest never will be) sunshine and roses – and living in a perpetual state of nirvana would probably become stifling and boring. By the time we've reached midlife, we've all faced our challenges – some of us having more than others, and some of us having far more than our fair share. Courage and resilience, however, come from our ability to get back up again after we've tripped and fallen over on life's obstacle course. Getting back up again is a choice – and we always have that choice.

So, we get to midlife – and we face transition. Those of us who are parents come to realise that our children do not rely on us as they once did and they are leaving home. Those of us who have been homemakers for many years may wonder, 'Who am I now? What is my role?' And our parents are ageing, we have health scares, and our friends have health scares.

Some of us may well be troubled with thoughts that the person sitting opposite us (and the one with whom we've lived for twenty or more years) isn't the one we remember falling in love with. Some of us are facing separation and divorce and learning to date all over again, some of us have become disillusioned with our work life, and still others are looking for brand-new careers.

We can face all these challenges with heavy hearts and resentment – or we can embrace this new phase in our lives with enthusiasm and vigour. This can be a time of renaissance for us: it can literally be our rebirth.

As for me, I would find myself looking in the mirror, wondering who that woman was who was looking back at me. She looked familiar, yet I did not quite recognise her. Perhaps there was something in her eyes that reminded me of someone I once knew . . . Was she someone I loved and cared for deeply? She looked like someone I ought to become reacquainted with, someone I needed to rediscover.

My story began one miserable day when I was nursing a broken heart. Years of tears and grief came flooding out of me. Tears and grief that were, truth be told, decades old. I'm just grateful I had children at home and a reason to rise every day, because I don't know how long I might have stayed under the covers listening to heart-breaking love songs and wallowing in my grief.

A text came in from a girlfriend asking how I was. I responded that I was wretched and didn't know how I would be able to get any semblance of a happy life together again. She texted me back with the words, *All I can say is it gets better. Go gently, be kind to yourself, and best knickers always.*

Oh my dear, sweet, lovely friend knew exactly what I needed to hear at that precise moment. She knew because she too had been there. The sad thing was that I had stopped looking after myself, stopped being kind to myself and my self-esteem had taken quite a beating. The lingerie I always prided myself on was nowhere to be seen, banished to the back of the drawer.

I understood exactly what my friend meant by her text. She wanted me to care for myself – to nurture and look after myself. I was, of course, doing nothing of the sort; I was neglecting myself. I've always gone by the credo that if my hair is cut and I have mascara on (and perhaps a little lipstick), I'm ready to face the world. But there I was, forgetting even these small attentions that I'd always regarded as my bare necessities.

It was time to start looking after *me* again.

Time moved on. Slowly I healed. I sat early one morning on my deck, coffee in hand, in unseasonably warm sunshine. And as I absorbed the peace of my surroundings, some questions came to me.

How had I managed to turn my life around?

What had I done to change where I had been four years before to get me to where I was today?

Back then I had been battling with a deeply troubled

marriage, a son leaving home for university, another son desperately unhappy in school, and my daughter and husband had serious health issues. And that was before I acknowledged the scars I myself had from ten years of depression. I felt somehow that I was living in a coma, functioning day-to-day inside a deep well of sadness and malaise. I was in a black hole with no sight of daylight.

And yet . . . surely there had to be more to life?

I picked up my journal and pen and wrote.

This is my renaissance.

The Lessons

LESSON 1

Start from where you are

So many times we sit paralysed because of fear or regret. I learned to stop wishing things were different. I came to realise that my life had got to this point for a reason; that it had been necessary to get to rock bottom in order to start building strong and solid foundations for a brighter future. I needed to start from where I was; wishing things were different wasn't going to help me in any way at all. If anything, those wishes would hold me back and delay my healing.

At times I would wish I'd made different choices. I would regret things I had either done or not done and I would sit frozen to the spot, unable to think or see with any clarity, unable to move. My head ached from wishing, from over-thinking and it was getting me nowhere. Over time, and with guidance, I learned to stop wanting things to be different. My life was the way it was, however much I wished it were different.

The more I resisted and fought against accepting the situation, the more entangled I became. The more hopeless seemed the situation, the more helpless I felt. Accepting that I was where I was is the first step for me.

I clearly remember listening to myself complaining about my situation yet again to a friend –and frankly I was bored rigid, bored with the same old sob story, bored sick of feeling crap. I decided in that instant – don't worry, it wasn't an overnight miraculous transformation in my thinking, there were plenty more 'instants' – that my life had got me to where I was for a reason and I could either stay stuck or I could start from where I was; which at that time meant rock bottom. The beauty about rock bottom, of course, is that we get to build solid foundations (that's the joy of hindsight too because rock bottom doesn't feel like the kind of place you want to be joyful). So there I was, turning what had been a horrid situation into a lesson. Wishing things were different wasn't miraculously improving my life – I had to put the work in myself. Acceptance of a situation is a great lesson.

- *Starting from where you are, what can* you *do today?*

LESSON 2

You are more courageous than you believe

We take so much of our strength and resilience for granted. Courage isn't about being a battle-ready soldier; some days there is courage in saying, 'tomorrow is another day'. We show courage on a daily basis because our lives and the lives of those we love matter to us. When we feel deeply passionate about something, we find courage easily – for example, we find superhuman strength to protect our children. So let us find that same passion and courage for ourselves, trusting that whatever our circumstances are right now (and regardless of whether we feel courageous), we can find a valuable seam of courage if we dig just below the surface.

I've kept this quote by Mary Anne Radmacher close to my heart, 'Courage doesn't always roar. Sometimes courage is the quiet voice at the end of the day that says "I will try again tomorrow."'

I have been called courageous, resilient and brave many times in my life (I've also been called foolhardy, naive and delusional – see Lesson 28 about editing your Friendship List!), I was asked one day by a friend, 'How do you do it? I just don't have your courage.' I thought about it when I got home, I didn't see myself as particularly courageous, but it got me thinking about the meaning of courage and what it meant to me and I wrote down these thoughts in my journal:

- Courage is saying 'I'm sorry'.
- Courage is knowing when to say 'enough'.
- Courage is saying 'I love you'.
- Courage is saying 'yes'.

- Courage is saying 'no'.
- Courage is being truthful with oneself.
- Courage is knowing that we screwed up.
- Courage is admitting we can't cope alone.
- Courage is letting go.
- Courage is reaching out.
- Courage is standing up for something we believe in.
- Courage is burning bridges and never going back.
- Courage is doing something new.
- Courage is being willing to receive.
- Courage is trusting someone again.
- Courage is choosing love over fear.
- Courage is standing up for oneself.
- Courage is choosing to truly live.
- Courage is learning to love again.
- Courage is believing in oneself for the first time.
- Courage is being vulnerable.
- Courage is breaking with tradition.
- Courage is asking for help.
- Courage is stopping to rest.
- Courage is letting the tears flow.
- Courage is continuing through adversity.
- Courage is trusting that all will be well.

- *What is the smallest possible step* you *could take to believe in your own courage?*

LESSON 3

Surround yourself with warriors

My journey was made possible because of the extraordinary women and men in my life who love me for who I am – they are my mentors and my cheerleaders. Allow these people into your life to give you the love and support that you deserve. Reach out to those loyal friends who will stand in your corner and fight for you when you feel you cannot take another step.

There have been plenty of days when I wasn't sure if I had the strength to go on. There were days when I would literally crawl upstairs to bed on my hands and knees because my legs would no longer carry me. The tough days were really tough, both physically and emotionally, whether it was confronting my daughter's anorexia or sitting in the mediator's office to face another round of heavy divorce negotiations. It was my warrior friends who supported me with their words and with their practical help. A little like the Footprints in the Sand prayer in which, rather than being deserted when our load is too great, God (and in my case, friends) carry us: this is the time that we are cradled by our loved ones. I was never abandoned because my problems were too great for anyone to bear, I was carried when I couldn't walk on my own.

Food would be left on my doorstep; texts arrived letting me know just how important I was in someone's life; phone calls in the morning checked that I was up. I am filled with such love and gratitude for these warriors, although some were not so gentle and would give me a good kick up the backside. They would show me my value by not accepting less than I was worth and they held me together when my self-esteem and self-worth were dragging on the floor. They kept a candle alight when I was lost in the dark. One of my warriors made me a silver bangle with the word 'FEARLESS' stamped on it. I wear it every day as a reminder that I, too, am a warrior in someone else's life in return.

• *Who are the warriors in* your *life?*

LESSON 4

Don't bury your rage and anger

I grew up with an inability to express anger. Anger was not approved of. I buried all my feelings of anger and throughout this journey would turn rage in on myself. With the support of a loving friend, I learned to accept that my anger was valid and that the psychological pain would diminish if I released it. It is important to express anger and find a way to release it safely. Try kick-boxing, going out into nature and screaming at the top of your voice, or looking into EFT (Emotional Freedom Technique).

Anger is an emotion that many of us are afraid of, an emotion that can be seen in its extreme as violent and ugly. It is an emotion that can escalate quickly. But why did I get angry? I guess it came from not being 'heard', not being listened to and not being understood. I would feel that what I had to say was of no value. Anger and expressing my anger was not something that I have ever found easy. My response to anger had always been to cry. I felt trapped, I would feel humiliated by my inarticulacy. As someone who finds expressing myself easy, when I felt angry I would collapse internally and cry. This was often interpreted as emotional blackmail but it was because I felt I had nowhere else to go and the tears would simply roll down my cheeks at my own frustration. I used to be frightened of the reaction of those around me if I said the words 'I'm angry' and so people became defensive. What could have been a debate or a heated discussion would end up with one or the other party going silent and/or in tears. The pressure of unsaid words or unexpressed emotion would give me a physical pain in my chest and the anger was turned inside to fester. I still won't actively choose confrontation, yet thankfully I have explored my anger and frustration from the past, come to terms with it and accepted it, so now I am happy to say that I'm angry, knowing that the world won't fall apart.

- *How do you express and deal with anger?*

LESSON 5

Count your blessings

Showing gratitude is part of my daily practice. However bad things are, there is always something – even just one small thing – for which we can be grateful. For a long time I kept a notebook by my bedside and, each night before falling asleep, I would jot down a handful of things for which I was grateful and then would think about these as I fell asleep. Sometimes, when the going was particularly tough, I struggled to find anything to be grateful for, but even at those times I could eventually find gratitude for a warm bed or food in my stomach or a goodnight kiss from one of my children. I believe it was these tiny, almost inconsequential, things that kept me going.

I am a firm believer in giving thanks and being grateful. I was raised a Catholic and although I no longer adhere to formal religion, I have positive memories as a young child of kneeling by the side of my bed with my parents and sister and saying our evening prayers. 'Thank you, Jesus, for a lovely day, God bless Mummy, Daddy, Rebecca and Bridget and all our family and friends.' These days my beliefs are more spiritual in nature, yet I continue to give thanks daily for all I have in my life. Sometimes in a notebook, sometimes out loud, sometimes in a text or an email and sometimes directly onto my iPhone app.

As I raised my own children, I taught them to be grateful too. Thank you was said for meals before they left the table, thank-you notes were written for gifts, thank you was said to a friend's mum before leaving the play date. Simple manners, yes, but they were also learning to show gratitude.

I have found that saying thank you and showing gratitude comes naturally and I feel blessed. And when I feel blessed I feel more open and happier.

Gratitude heals our wounds. Call me crazy, but I'm also sincerely grateful for the tough times, for the long, dark days and nights. I am grateful for the lessons they taught me. Without them I would not be the woman I am today and for that I am deeply grateful.

- *Who and what are* you *most grateful for in your life?*

LESSON 6

Take time for time out

'Let us be silent, that we may hear the whispers of the gods', Ralph Waldo Emerson taught us. We live in a noisy world.

There was a lot of noise in my head and I longed for silence in a mad world. I have taken up meditation again, and this time I am guided in my daily practice. I take twenty minutes simply to sit and be aware of my breathing, allowing thought to come and go. I focus on my intention for my meditation. I have learned to take time out for solitude and self-reflection. It is a healing remedy for the mind, body and soul.

A wise friend once asked me, 'How often do you allow yourself to experience *real* solitude? I mean time that you consciously choose to spend alone? Time that you've carved out purely for yourself?'

Infrequently to never, was my response. As someone rarely alone, like so many of us who give of ourselves to others in our work and our family lives, creating times of solitude seemed like an impossible task. Therefore, if we are to do so, we must do it with determination. Even those of us who live alone can fill our time with busyness and ignore the very real benefits of consciously being in solitude.

Taking some time in solitude enabled me to press pause on the chaos in my life, it's a bit like pressing pause on the treadmill at the gym and standing on the sides watching the machine still running below.

Taking some time out means:

- We give ourselves the chance to think about our lives in greater depth.
- We can take some time for contemplation and self-reflection.
- We notice and become aware of the world around us.
- We become more creative in our thinking, we begin to see possibilities rather than problems.
- We learn to step back and de-stress by slowing down for a while.

Solitude needn't be about sitting in the lotus position meditating. Here are some things that I do when I choose to have reflective time on my own.

- I keep a journal – sometimes I write my pages in the morning, sometimes whilst I'm having my lunch or a coffee break.
- I walk in my local park at a time when I'm least likely to bump into people.
- I wake early and now no longer fight it – I enjoy the stillness of the house as I spend time reflecting on the day ahead.
- I go to bed early in order to read or to write or to day-dream.

Sometimes these moments need to be snatched, even if it means locking the bathroom door to soak in the bath or paint our toenails without interruption, or walking the dog around the block for ten minutes.

Time in solitude is vital to my sanity.

- *What activities or thought encourage a sense of peace for you?*

You are the only one standing in your way

I battled for a long time with my own demons. I got into the blame game. It was my husband or my parents or my school teacher or my boss . . . and then I realised that it was me. No one but me was stopping me from making choices for my life. I decided to get out of my way and move towards creating a brighter, inspiring, more fulfilling life. Take a long, hard look at the person you see in the mirror and ask yourself: what if I were to stop the excuses and get out of my own way?

As a coach I often watch my clients battling with barriers they have erected that prevent them from moving forward in life. I watch as they barricade themselves inside their self-limiting world. I hear excuses for why something cannot be achieved or done and they are all self-imposed. It's self-sabotage. And yes, I do it myself. But remember:

- Self-sabotage is a dream stealer.
- Self-sabotage leads us to eat another piece of cake.
- Self-sabotage urges us to open the bottle of wine.
- Self-sabotage chooses rotten partners for us.
- Self-sabotage says it's too cold and wet and dark to go to the gym.
- Self-sabotage stops us applying for that great job.
- Self-sabotage is a bitch. It keeps us trapped within our comfort zone.

Why?

Because the voice that we so often hear and the voice I heard time and time again was: 'Because I don't deserve it. Because I'm not worth it.'

Why do we allow this 'voice' to prevent us from doing what we want to do? What frightens us? What is the reason behind self-sabotage that causes us to retreat into our shell, to play small?

Is it fear of success? Fear that life might actually turn out really well? Are we afraid of having what we really want in life?

I know self-sabotage well.

- Self-sabotage manifests itself in opening the fridge to pour a glass of wine because 'I need to unwind' (even though I've committed to myself that I won't do it, it only makes me fall asleep).

- Self-sabotage manifests in making all sorts of excuses not to go to the gym even though I know how good I feel after the burn.
- Self-sabotage manifests in procrastination – somehow the ironing has more appeal than applying for a new job.
- Self-sabotage manifests in over-analysing a text from my man rather than enjoying the relationship.
- Self-sabotage keeps us small and living unfulfilled lives.

What was I prepared to do about self-sabotage? How was I going to get out of my own way? By trying as hard as I could not to do any of the above.

- *How are* you *being the main obstacle on your path?*

LESSON 8

We all have a choice

Remember that even deciding to do nothing is a choice. And even though we might feel that circumstances are beyond our control and that we really do not have a choice, we *always* have a choice in our attitude towards a situation. I am inspired by Viktor Frankl, the psychiatrist and Holocaust survivor who wrote in his book *Man's Search for Meaning*: 'Everything can be taken from a man but one thing: the last of the human freedoms – to choose one's attitude in any given set of circumstances, to choose one's own way.' His words give me the lift and the courage to behave differently. If we say we have no choice, we become a victim to our circumstances.

Yes, I *did* have a choice. Even though things seemed at times to be happening outside my control (and still do) I did, and do, have a choice. I can choose my response to the situation. This applies to everything: I could choose my attitude. Yes, this takes a leap of faith. Did I want to stamp my feet and rage? Yes.

Turmoil? Anger? Frustration? Overwhelmed? Instead of drowning in it, I could choose a different attitude and rise above it. I could choose to make myself miserable or I could choose to have a different attitude. In choosing a different response, I was choosing my own way and leaving the role of victim to be played by others.

Surely what was 'troubling' me, whatever turmoil I was in, whatever grief I was 'suffering', I could master with a change in attitude?

• *How would a change in attitude benefit you?*

LESSON 9

Be open-minded and stop judging

Are you always right? Is your way the only way? Do you notice yourself judging people because of the way they look or behave? Are you intolerant generally? Do you criticise freely and easily? We have no idea what others are going through or why they behave the way they do. Let's put ourselves in their shoes whenever we feel ourselves judging. And what about ourselves? Let's stop that self-critical and condemning voice once and for all, shall we?

In my world, empathy is the opposite of judgment. If I can empathise with someone, with their views, with their values, I don't need to agree with them but it gets me a closer understanding of their life. In learning to have compassion for someone else I can then begin to be compassionate with myself. When I judge others, I judge myself.

This is something that took time for me to fully understand. I'd got used to judging myself: I wasn't good enough, clever enough, lovable enough and I wasn't happy because of this exhausting judging. My coach asked me to keep a log of every time I judged myself and make a note of it — and it scared me how rubbish my self-talk was. Slowly I came to realise that it wasn't going to help me become my best self. It was time to let go of this constant judging

I saw a great tweet recently, a quote from Pastor Steven Furtick: 'The reason we struggle with insecurity is because we compare our behind-the-scenes with everyone else's highlight reel.'

In letting go of judgment we learn to forgive, which is surely one of the greatest gifts. In learning not to judge – and hence forgive – I am able (most of the time) to be free of the negative talk that comes my way from some people.

- *Would* you *allow a friend to speak about herself the way you speak about yourself?*

LESSON 10

Don't be a martyr

Ever, ever, ever! Stop it right now. It's game-playing, and you are so much better than that. I feel very strongly about this. Martyrdom was a big part of my life (and the lives of many women I know). I used to get some sick pleasure out of behaving in this way, of making others suffer and feel my pain. It was shameful. And then one day I stopped, just like that.

You can simply decide to stop, too.

It was one of those get-really-honest-with-yourself moments during my coaching course, a time to get down and dirty with the parts of ourselves that we don't actually like. I'm not talking body parts, but the bits of our character, the sides to us that prevent us growing. Little Miss Need to be Perfect was one, and Little Miss Not Quite Good Enough, Little Miss I'm SO Busy, Little Miss Controlled Anger . . . but the winner was The Martyr. My great big, Joan of Arc-burning-at-the-stake martyr and that's actually how I drew her on paper. Oh, I was an excellent martyr. It worked every time. 'Oh don't worry, I'll do it,' I said with a sigh. 'No, you have the last piece of chocolate cake, I shouldn't really anyway,' said with a passive voice. 'You go and sit down, I'll do the dishes and the tidying up and put the washing on and walk the dog and do the shopping . . . ' 'I don't mind' . . . and so it went on.

Don't you just hate it when someone close to you is being a martyr? That was me. And there I was, owning up to the group in full Technicolor, risking them seeing me with fresh eyes. But in owning up, my very own Joan of Arc lost her power.

Being a martyr disempowers; it weakens us both physically and mentally and it was a badge I didn't want to wear any longer. I urge you to take it off too.

- *Be honest, when was the last time* you *acted the martyr?*

LESSON 11

Do the thing that scares you

We grow when we move out of our comfort zone. Take a risk. Write that letter. Tell that person you love her/him. Go for that job. Life might feel safe, but isn't safety oh so boring? I promise you, you'll feel strong, empowered, and alive for that little stretch. The inspiring Eleanor Roosevelt encourages us: 'You gain strength, courage, and confidence by every experience in which you stop to look fear in the face. You are able to say to yourself, "I lived through this horror. I can take the next thing that comes along." The danger lies in refusing to face the fear, in not daring to come to grips with it. If you fail anywhere along the line, it will take away your confidence. You must make yourself succeed every time. You must do the thing you think you cannot do.'

What scared me? To stand in my kitchen, to ask for a divorce and say out loud: 'I don't want to live like this any more.' It terrified me and, at the same time, it liberated me. On the other side of fear is a whole new world. I did what I thought I could not do and I survived.

This whole 'life begins at the end of your comfort zone' isn't strictly true. Life just *is*, whether you're in or out of your comfort zone it just depends how alive and fulfilled you choose to be. Life in my comfort zone was okay: it was safe, it was easy, it was risk-free – but, in all honesty, it wasn't joyful, exciting or that enjoyable. It was, in many respects, a life lived inauthentically. I wasn't living truthfully. I had forgotten who I was. Yes, I was mother and wife and sister and daughter and loyal friend, but who was I, Rebecca?

I needed and desperately wanted to take that risk, I wanted to think and act for myself, to quieten the voices of those around me and those in my head. I wanted to believe in myself and in my courage.

So here I am on the other side of that fear, alive, vibrant, pursuing a new career and life – all because I faced what I needed to face, one step at a time, surrounded by my warriors.

- *What is the cost to* you *of playing it safe?*

LESSON 12

Be opinionated

Stand up for what you believe in. I think it's something we get better at as we get older. There is value in saying, 'I don't know' when you really mean it, and there's a wonderful sense of curiosity attached to it. But, damn it, stand up for your beliefs and your opinions – even if they run counter to what everyone else believes.

There was a time when I was a bit of a mouse. I grew up without voicing my opinion. I guess what I was scared of was that what I had to say wouldn't be seen as valuable or worthwhile or, worse still, would be laughed at. I was fearful of rejection, so I kept my mouth shut.

I'm not political in any way, yet I have a strong set of values that I live by, my moral code. If someone is going to violate my values then I will let them know, not in an aggressive and angry way, but in a way that lets them know my opinions. I have become more forthright.

It's taken a lot of courage and belief in myself to stand up for what I feel is right. I see many women around me who are finally finding their voice in midlife. Women who will no longer be silenced. Women who are finding their feet again. Women who want to be heard. Women who are standing up for justice. Women who are finding courage and strength from deep inside. I like it.

- *Do you believe what* you *have to say is of value?*

LESSON 13 •

Listen to and trust your intuition

We so often doubt ourselves. We listen more to what others think or say than to ourselves, yet there's this aching in the back of our minds, a knowing and an inclination toward the right choice. Often, we must make a wrong decision to realise that listening to our own intuition would have led us to better things. So have courage, because you have a deep wisdom. No one said it would be easy to trust our intuition, and it can be a long, hard road, but when a choice feels right for you, pursue it.

I knew I no longer wanted to be a passive onlooker in life. I wanted to be courageous, take risks and lead a more fulfilling life. Intuitively, I knew this, had known it for many years, yet I kept coming up with reasons for not living fully and with purpose.

What would others say? What would my family feel? What if I was laughed at, scorned? What if people turned their backs on me?

I asked myself what I was teaching my children of love and life and living if I was not living life being true to myself? What was I currently teaching them about life? That life simply happens to us or we are able to make conscious and enlightened choices? I knew, within my well of sadness, that I would have to make the choice for my children to experience pain – the pain that, for their parents, there was to be no 'and they lived happily ever after'. We were to become a 'broken family'. At the same time I knew – and held on to this belief, desperately at times – that life would be so much better afterwards, once we'd all come through the pain, once their parents were no longer causing each other hurt.

Trusting our intuition is oftentimes challenging as it begs of us to take 'the road less travelled', to head down a path with no signposts: we are asked to simply trust our inner compass.

- *What do you intuitively know is right for* you?

LESSON 14

Laugh until our face aches

Laughing is contagious. Laughing relieves stress. We all know how good we feel when we laugh. So have as much fun as you possibly can. Make room for frivolity in your life. Remain childlike. See the funny side to life. Surround yourself with people you can have a good laugh with. Learn to enjoy laughing at yourself, too. Don't be too precious.

Life, for me, had just got so flipping serious. Nothing made me laugh. Life was one long, hard slog.

There are some crazy statistics about how many times a day a child laughs and how few times we do as adults . . .

I rediscovered laughing (sounds mad!) when I was training to be a coach. I met some of my now-closest friends on those courses. We were all going through the same questioning of ourselves whilst studying and perhaps it was because we were all in this together that we felt freer together. We had no previous history, we had no prior connections, we simply got on and connected freely and easily. During evenings spent in the pub or over coffee breaks, crazy life stories began to be shared. I learned to laugh again, to laugh with others and to laugh at myself.

I was reminded of this just the other day. I had spent the morning with two friends whom I hadn't seen for a while. It was a spontaneous meeting up, no expectations. One of my friends is an extraordinary storyteller and, wonderfully, she has no idea just how perfectly she shares her stories, recounting her life. She sends herself up in the most delightful way, stories told at top speed with a smattering of expletives. I could barely breathe by the end for laughing so much, tears streaming down my face, my arms clutching my stomach, my cheeks aching. Oh, the delight and the joy.

Laughing heals us. Laughing takes years off us. Stuff the crow's feet – I'm happy developing laughter lines.

• *What truly makes* you *laugh?*

LESSON 15

Start by changing one thing in your life

We are creatures of habit and habits can sometimes lead to boredom and stagnation. Learning to get a different perspective in life means that we can begin to make changes as we look at our lives differently. Start today. Make one small, positive change and see what happens. Drive a different way to work, set your alarm ten minutes earlier so that you're not rushing, drink herbal tea instead of reaching for another coffee.

There is something exhilarating about making positive change in our life. It could simply be making the decision to look after ourselves a little more, to start going to the gym, to cut out the caffeine. Making changes can happen one at a time and then, all of a sudden, you turn around and see just how far you've come. Congratulate yourself: you'll have already done more than most people do who get stuck in the *talking* about making changes.

Admittedly, for me the one thing I changed was one huge thing. But don't be fooled; it had taken a long time of small changes, often internal, self-talk changes, before I was able to make the change I wanted. The story I wanted to tell of my life when I'm old is the one that goes: I faced my fear, I said I wanted a divorce, the world kept on turning and I lived – and *am* living – the life I chose to live from that day on.

* *What story will you want to tell about your life when you're old?*

LESSON 16

Question your beliefs

How often do you hear someone else's words coming out of your own mouth? How often do you do things because you've always done them? I began to question my beliefs and found that I no longer held many of them to be true, because they had never been my beliefs in the first place. I choose to believe in myself rather than the dogma of the church in which I was raised. Today I choose to believe that I am clever enough, and wise enough, and good enough, just as I am. I do not need anyone else's opinion or beliefs about what I can or can't or should or shouldn't do. Perhaps this is one of the gifts that midlife brings. It's liberating once we let go of others' beliefs, as they are usually the ones that limit us – as Walt Whitman wrote: 'Re-examine all you have been told . . . dismiss what insults your soul.'

Funny, isn't it, how we believe and take as fact much of what we're told when we're young? I grew up with the words of my English teacher resonating in my head.

I remember as if it were yesterday the sheer humiliation I felt, aged twelve, when my teacher slammed my exercise book onto the desk in front of the whole class. How is it, she said, that I shone in French, Latin and Welsh but that in English I showed 'absolutely no imagination'. How those words stung. Little did I know then that what we focus our thoughts on, that those things we spend our life thinking about, become our reality. You see, I went on to agree with and fulfil that teacher's belief of me. And that belief that I lacked the right words, the right imagination, in my native language, led to some catastrophic failures in my English lessons in school – even as I passed every other subject with flying colours.

Fast-forward thirty years to a coach training course in London. It came at a time in my life when I felt timid and found myself wrestling with insecurity. I'd had a tough few years and felt very much like the twelve-year-old me in front of my English teacher.

And yet, this image is not one that others saw in me. 'Are you a writer?' I was asked again and again. Was I an author? A journalist?

Me?

'Oh, no,' I replied. 'You see, I can't write. Good lord, no. I've never even kept a diary.' In spite of my objections, the people I met through my coaching experiences kept making observations like: 'You always seem to have just the right words to say.' 'You sum things up eloquently and succinctly.'

Why was it, then, that I'd never seen myself as one who creates with words?

And just like that I banished the words of my old teacher (who was probably only having a bad day) and my new career began.

- *What beliefs about yourself are* you *willing to question and change?*

Love with all your heart

My favourite Beatles song is 'All You Need is Love'. Imagine a world filled with love. With love we thrive. There is so much love – passionate love, unrequited love, familial love, love for our children, love we would lay down our very lives for, love for our neighbour, and compassionate love for another. Until we love and hold ourselves in esteem, how can we truly love and allow another to show us love? Be open and big-hearted. Be ready to express and show love. It is so easy to crawl into our shell when we've been hurt and have had some hard knocks. I know; I've done it. It takes courage to fall in love again. Can I guarantee you won't get hurt? No. Is it worth it? Yes.

I was looking for love outside of myself. But to love and believe in myself was what had to happen first. Until then, why would anyone else love and believe in me?

I had become fearful of love. I gave it freely, too freely perhaps, and I allowed myself to be hurt. I had developed serious attachment problems. At the time I believed that being loved by someone else would solve all my problems. I believed that 'we' would conquer the world. There was, of course, no 'us'. I was needy and clingy and overwhelmingly desperate to be loved.

The truth was that I needed to love myself, to completely love the woman I was. Why was I looking for love outside of myself? In hindsight, what I was demanding of this man was a love I was unable to show myself. I was expecting my first post-marriage love affair to complete me, to make me whole. We are fed this message in all the disempowering love songs we listen to on the radio and I was expecting him to fill the void within me, to accept and love me even though I was unable to accept and love myself. Heavy going, right?

My heart broke when our relationship ended and my life was shattered. But it needed to happen, and it was good that it happened, for it allowed deep healing within my life. The tears were cathartic. The tears healed my fears of being unworthy of love. Little by little, and with the support of a therapist as well as good friends, I healed my old wounds. I began to love myself for who I was. I learned to allow love into my life again. This time a love based on mutual respect, of understanding of each other without neediness. I am now able to answer the question, 'Do I love myself, truly and deeply, just as I am?' with the answer 'Yes, and I continue to learn to do so.'

- *Do* you *love yourself? Truly and deeply, just as you are?*

LESSON 18

'If you're going through hell, keep going'

The quote above is attributed to Winston Churchill and is believed to relate to his depression. Whether he said it or not, how this quote kept me strong! Even in the darkest moments I had a sense that it was easier to keep moving forward than turning back or giving up. Depression is not about feeling sad. It is not about feeling a bit down or being in a bad mood. Depression is a blackness. Depression sucks all emotion from us. You are left feeling hollow and numb and with a deep sense of hopelessness and loneliness. Depression drains the world of its colour and sound and taste and smell.

Depression is a mental illness that, sadly, carries a huge stigma. It frustrates me that people are fearful of it, those with it and also society at large. If you have a heart condition, diabetes or a broken leg you wouldn't dream of not attending to it, of not taking advice from experts on how to repair the damage. No one is going to call you weak if you are unable to fix your broken leg. Then why is it that so often I hear people saying they won't see a professional therapist in order to gain an insight into their troubled minds, or they won't take medication for depression to help them begin to make sense of where they are?

I have experienced some very black and bleak places in my mind. I spent some of my teenage years with depression. I suffered chronic postnatal depression and I suffered again as I was battling with a deteriorating marriage. There were days when I could barely get out of bed and went around in some sort of coma. I would have panic attacks collecting the children from school and couldn't face anyone, especially those closest to me. At times I couldn't even speak, such was my fear of opening the floodgates of my tears. I lost a huge amount of weight, developed asthma, and I had tonsillitis permanently. Simple, everyday tasks became my very own Everest – and still I battled on.

I have invested time getting myself to where I am today. I have taken medication and I have spent many hours with a variety of therapists – and all these helped me piece my life back together again. Today, I know the triggers and I know how to handle them. I have been well for over a decade. That's not to say that I live my life in a perpetual blissful state. I'm realistic, yet I won't let a 'blue' day affect me in the devastating way it used to.

- *What mantra or affirmation keeps* you *going forward when life is tough?*

LESSON 19

Every cloud has a silver lining

We may not know it at the time – and in all likelihood we never fully appreciate it at the time – but there is a reason for the way things turn out. We hear people say that becoming seriously ill was the best thing that happened to them once they've recovered. We hear people saying that a divorce, however painful, turned out to be a good thing. We hear people say that losing a job was exactly what was needed to launch a business. So believe in silver linings.

I learned to hold on to these two age-old truths: the sun always follows the rain and there is blue sky behind even the darkest of clouds. I am always much happier outdoors. I long for the spring when the heating can go off and the windows and doors can be left open. I love changing the air in the house.

I knew the dark clouds of my life would lift at some point. I knew that at some point I would hold dearly the lessons I was learning about life and love and pain and suffering (mine and the pain I was causing). My silver lining to these dark clouds was that I trusted and believed, deeply, that the sun would come out after the rain. Life would be better once we got through the downpour. And yes, I'm happy to say that, although divorce was something I chose to bring into our family, it is good that it happened. Fear of the pain it would cause to those around me was no reason not to go through the pain. I did it consciously as I believed life would be better on the other side. And the sun *did* come out.

- *What is* your *silver lining?*

LESSON 20

Learn to listen

Be less eager to talk – real listening is a beautiful thing and to be truly heard by another is a gift. We feel validated and important. Sadly, most people don't listen; they are simply waiting to talk. You see it in their eyes and their body language. Don't be one of those people. Stop and listen and others will always remember how you made them feel.

'Out of the mouths of babes . . .' the psalm goes. I was busy stressing in the kitchen, two of my children doing homework and my youngest around my ankles (well that's what it felt like). My mind was racing from thought to thought, catastrophising as usual. Somewhere in the background I was aware of my name being called; it was getting more and more insistent and I suddenly came to as if from a dream to realise that my son was pulling on my leg and calling my name. I had apparently been nodding and agreeing with the a-has and mmms that we do. He pulled me down to his level so that we were eye to eye. He stood in front of me frowning, his hands on my face and said the words I will always remember 'Mummy, will you just listen to me, please?' I lifted him up in my arms, fighting back the tears. I sat him on the worktop so we could still be eye to eye. I kissed him and knew in that moment that I was being taught a lesson. I learned the importance of listening from my child. We show respect and consideration for others when we listen. We empower them; we show them how much we value them.

- *Who would* you *benefit from listening to?*

LESSON 21

Have big dreams

What did you dream of? It's not too late, you know. Write down your wildest dreams. You'll be amazed at what you draw into your life in doing so. Even the biggest, wildest, seemingly impossible, maddest dreams begin with one step. What small step might you take today in the direction you want to go?

I have a journal and in it I write: 'I dream of . . .' and I fill it with big, wild, incredible and unimaginable dreams, dreams that make me laugh out loud with their audacity. Of course, it wasn't always like that. I grew up to be a pessimist, a 'realist' some would say. 'Think the worst and then you'll never be disappointed' was my attitude then. Well, I say NO to that now.

There's a bit of me that some of you might find rather New Agey, but bear with me. Be clear on your goals/dreams and write them down. Have a plan on how you'll achieve them . . . get on with life, believe to your bones that this or something better will happen. Tell someone, because we're not great at being accountable simply to ourselves and see what magic you can create. You tell me yours and I'll tell you mine

Too many of us put lids on our dreams because we don't want to 'get above our station'. We curtail our life plans as we focus on the toil of day-to-day life. Today I came across a wonderful Mary Ann Evans' (aka George Eliot) quote again: 'It is never too late to be what you might have been.' and it reminded me of a woman I know, who at seventy-five decided she wanted to make some positive changes in her life. Please don't let anyone ever tell you that you're too old to change.

• *What dreams did* you *give up on a long time ago?*

LESSON 22

Put together a playlist of your ultimate feel-good songs

This was one of the best things I did, I'd forgotten how wonderful it was to sing and dance in the privacy of my own kitchen. Play them when the blues strike and play them when you're feeling on top of the world. My playlist is entitled Best Knickers Always Kitchen Disco and you can find it at the back of this book.

When I was a student I played music all the time; I wore out cassettes by Roberta Flack, Aretha Franklin and George Benson. And then I think I grew up (or that's what it felt like), life became more serious and the only cassettes/CDs playing were the children's story tapes or nursery rhymes. I do remember dancing in the kitchen to The Gypsy Kings with my small children and those are very happy memories. Then I forgot about my music for a while. Maybe there was so much noise in my head I couldn't cope with anything more. And then music became my saviour, one song in particular, 'Smooth' by Carlos Santana with the voice of

Rob Thomas. I played this every time I needed to feel courageous, strong, empowered and brave. I hear it today and I walk taller, I move my body and I feel more me than ever before. The next song to touch me in this way was 'Sweet Home Alabama' by Lynyrd Skynyrd, which even made it as the ringtone on my phone and I'd need to listen to as much of it as I could before answering so it didn't go to voicemail. Curtis Mayfield was added to the now developing Best Knickers Always Playlist, 'Move On Up' he sang to me, 'remember your dream is your only scheme'. Oh yes, Mr Mayfield, I would play it loud. I would pour a glass of wine whilst I prepared supper and I'd dance and sing loudly with a wooden spoon in hand as a stand-in microphone. And you know what? Whatever kind of crap day I'd had, the sun would seem to come out, I'd get back in touch with the rhythm of my body and I'd smile. 'And I'm feeling good . . .' Thank you, Nina Simone, you're on there too.

- *What's on* your *ultimate feel-good playlist?*

LESSON 23

Decide what you are prepared to tolerate in your life

The boss who takes advantage? The partner who belittles you in front of other people? The children who walk all over you? The friend who talks behind your back? Decide what you will put up with so it's *your* choice and then stop moaning about what you *have* to put up with. Remember that it is you who allows this in your life: nobody does this to you without your permission.

When I was asked this question on my coaching course, I began a long list of things that I was tolerating – front door needs painting, in-tray over-full, no light bulb in the oven, receipts overflowing in my purse, kids leaving stuff on the stairs and wet towels on the floor, my procrastination, only me unloading the dishwasher and walking the dog . . . That's just a snapshot. The cost of tolerating these things was that I got stressed some more, I felt used and frustrated.

Was I being a doormat? Was it allowing me to avoid confrontation with the children? Who was suffering here? I prioritised the list and took action to begin tackling the ones I could do myself and came up with a plan with the children so I wasn't nagging and they were more aware.

It's surprising what happens once we consciously decide something.

- *What are* you *tolerating in your life right now?*

LESSON 24

Be less available

People will leave a message if it's that important. The majority of us have answering machines or voicemail, so use them. (I still need to listen to my own advice on this one, by the way!) We really don't need to leave another comment on Facebook, reply to the text whilst in the middle of lunch, or tweet our latest thought. This is an ongoing effort for me.

Were times easier and simpler thirty-odd years ago when we had no Internet, no mobile phones, no social media? When I left home for university back in 1981, I went to the other side of the country. There was one pay-phone between thirty students and we queued to make the required weekly phone call home. There was no privacy, no chance for quiet conversation. I studied French, so spent time in Nice and Paris and phone calls became even more irregular. Is our instant access to communication today a good or bad thing? Is it progress? I'm not so sure. Are my children more dependent because I'm on the end of the phone, which I always have with me? Have I made them so because I am always available?

Running my own business, it's very difficult to switch off and be less available. I want to be there for my clients, yet I am also very aware that having my phone ping at all hours/during dinner/watching a film is not conducive to a happy and relaxing family life.

Being a single parent, I got into the habit of having my phone on 24/7 in order that my children could contact me should they need to. Was that nurturing or nannying? I have, in the past, liked a text to let me know they had arrived home safely. I am very well aware that it has become a habit, and although I coach my clients on changing habits, it's one I myself have to work on. I am a work in progress and know that taking any time away and being disconnected is a challenge. Perhaps a holiday on a deserted island without WiFi is the answer.

- *What would it be like if* you *disconnected, even if just for a few hours over the weekend?*

LESSON 25

Cultivate green fingers

No excuses! Whether you have a balcony or a meadow, grow mint (for Pimms, Mojitos and tea), chamomile (to rub between your fingers for instant calm), lavender (for memories of hot holidays) and fragrant roses (my favourite is Mme Alfred Carriere).

I grew up with home-grown fruit and vegetables. In the summer my sister and I would choose the vegetables for dinner. It's only as an adult that I realised what a wonderful experience that was as I stood in the supermarket deciding over the over-packaged, perfectly formed and uniform carrots and peppers, vegetables that didn't look like they'd seen soil. I never found the time to turn over a corner of my garden for vegetable growing, but managed to get pots of herbs and summer vegetables on my deck instead.

I have a small garden now, and on the deck we have pots filled with herbs; any time I go into the garden I twist mint leaves between my fingers as I pick them for tea and rub chamomile and lavender in my hands to relax me. These are precious moments.

Planting, watching the seeds germinate, watering and feeding courgette or tomato plants is, for me, one of life's great pleasures. They grow quickly, I like that. There is something rooted in survival about cutting, cooking and eating vegetables I have grown. On a very fundamental level, I knew I could feed my children for the cost of a packet of seeds.

* *What would growing something teach you?*

LESSON 26

Walk barefoot whenever you can

There is something to be said for being 'grounded'. Being in contact with the earth, sand, grass, wood – even carpet. Taking my shoes off and walking barefoot connects me with my surroundings whether I am inside or out. In Pilates and yoga we begin by consciously planting our feet on the ground. It gives us balance, connectedness, and stability. I personally feel that stability mentally as well as physically.

I'm sitting here writing barefoot. I walk barefoot whenever I can. I grew up wanting to be barefoot all summer long. I loved, and still do love, the sensation of grass under my feet, dew-laden in the early morning, freshly cut that turns the soles of my feet green, and lush, long, end-of-the-day-warm grass. I remember as a child being on holiday in the South of France and hopping down to the beach carrying a small blow-up dinghy with my sister. The sand was scorching hot and we had to jump into the boat every now and then to allow our feet to cool down. It was a delicious sensation. I love the feel of cold tiles on the soles of my feet, the feel of a beautiful wool carpet. Barefoot, yet with brand-new socks on, is another wonderful sensation. At the end of the day, I love to take my shoes or boots off and connect once more with the ground. I feel safe and grounded and at peace.

Should I ever remarry, I shall do so barefoot on a beach. Small wonder my children call me a hippy!

• *What do* you *do to feel grounded and connected?*

Allow yourself to be human

We are all perfect in our imperfections. We ALL make mistakes, so cut yourself some slack. We allow those we love to make mistakes, to be human – so, as a dear friend challenged me, 'What makes *you* think that you're any different?' Being human is enough. Lighten up! Life is far too important to be taken seriously. Make mistakes, learn from them, and move on.

What was it about me that made me think that 'human' simply wasn't good enough? I worked so damned hard at being the perfect mother, the perfect housewife, the best friend, the best at everything I did. I never expected it in my friends and family, yet I had to be perfect. Oh, and it's so damned exhausting and frustrating. I still battle with it.

- Supper took a lot longer to prepare than I'd planned last night and it nearly sent me into a downward spin – the perfect-hostess gremlin rearing her ugly head.
- I'm not as fit as the woman next to me on the mat in the gym – does that make me less than perfect? It certainly felt it at the time.
- I can't provide my children with all the things I'd like to – does that make me a less-than-perfect mother? Feels like it sometimes. Do they love me any less? Of course not.

So what is good enough for me right now is that I've decided to get fit and it will take time; supper, when it arrived at the table, was delicious; my children, in reality, want for nothing – they have a roof over their heads, they have food on the table and, most importantly, the unconditional love of their mother. That is surely more than enough. The words of my daughter ring in my ears: 'Cool your beans, Mama Bear.'

- *What is good enough for* you *right now?*

LESSON 28

It's okay to edit your friendship list

I have culled my list of friends a number of times in my life. Funnily enough, the ones who don't survive are the same ones who don't accept or welcome my growth. 'You've changed,' those people have said, 'I don't recognise you any more.' They are the ones who don't like that I've stopped living my life by their limiting rules and beliefs. Remember the saying that friends come into our lives for a reason, a season, or a lifetime. It's okay to let some go, whatever anyone tells you. Spend your time with those who help you raise your game, those who lift you up, and those who love you no matter what.

I learned who my friends were when life got tough. Some amazing people came into my life as others left when my life went into freefall. I have been criticised many times by some who see me 'abandoning' certain relationships. I have been called unpleasant names. I'm okay with that. Doors will always be left ajar for renewal or healing, should that be the right thing to do. Life is short. People change and not always at the same time. Relationships do need nurturing, this is true, yet sometimes, and often at a time of crisis, the people you have shared good times with cannot deal with the bad times. These do not make bad people, or bad friendships. It's simply a time to reassess the friendship/relationship and decide whether your values coincide any longer.

Surely friendships are to be enriching and not draining, and some friendships that had faded had become exhausting. I would come away feeling worse about life and myself – and at a time when life was pretty tough anyway, I no longer wanted that type of friendship. Of course it's easier to support those who are having a tough time when you're feeling good yourself. We all grow and change as we get older and for friendships and relationships to last, growth needs to happen, not necessarily simultaneously, but for there to be at least an understanding of the others' needs. True friends don't judge each other. There are many ex-friends who are no doubt relieved that I am no longer in their lives too.

- *Who are* you *trying to please?*

LESSON 29

Sex and orgasm

Yes! Yes! Yes! Much research has been done on the health benefits of orgasm; the pluses range from longevity to a reduction in the risk of breast cancer and heart disease. Orgasm has powerful analgesic effects. Sex burns calories. Orgasm reduces stress due to the release of oxytocin. We sleep better after an orgasm, the release of endorphins can have a sedative effect. Spice up your life a little (or a lot), write your own sexual fantasy, read some great erotica (the old stuff's the best), pay a visit to your local or online sex toy shop. Have some fun.

One of the many surreal moments in my life was when I stood in my local Ann Summers' shop discussing vibrators with a young sales assistant who could have been no older than my daughter. Have you had that experience? I'd experienced the joys of sex again after a hiatus of maybe four years and, oh boy, I liked it. Orgasm felt good. I slept better, I felt less stress in my life, I liked the spring it gave me in my step and the glow to my face. And apparently I looked younger. I wanted more. I wanted to be Sally Albright shouting out 'Yes, Yes, Yes'. It was time to go out exploring and make a purchase. I had never owned a vibrator – is that a sad admission at forty-five plus? Are the younger generation more enlightened or had it more to do, perhaps, with my strict upbringing?

So there I was, standing in front of a table of Rampant Rabbits with my eyes popping out of their sockets, asking this young, confident, and extremely knowledgeable sales assistant about the differences between them all apart from size and colour. I was part-entranced and part-squeamish. And then she said the magic words 'pelvic floor'.

'I'm sorry,' I said, 'did you just say that this one will work my pelvic floor whilst giving me a mind-blowing orgasm? I'll take it, thank you, and whilst you're at it I'll take another two as I know just the friends these are destined for . . . that'll shock them!'

- *Isn't it time to rediscover the pleasures, whether with a partner or solo? What will you try?*

LESSON 30

Take one step at a time

As with achieving any big dream, moving from where we are to where we'd like to be does not happen in giant leaps most of the time. It is, rather, the hundreds of baby steps we take that constitute our 'giant leaps' forward. My friend, a mountain guide, taught me this principle. She is an expert in the baby steps that lead to summit victories. As the Chinese proverb says, 'One step at a time is good walking.'

So what do you want to do now, that you'll do every day to live the life you want?

For a long time I was focused on problems rather than solutions. I wasn't ready, I'd say, the time wasn't right, I needed more information . . . but these were simply excuses that focused on why something wouldn't work out and I was delaying living the life I dreamed of because of this backlog of excuses and so-called reasons.

We all do it, don't we?

- When the children have left home.
- When I've lost weight.

- When I'm back in shape.
- After the summer holidays.
- When I'm feeling less tired.
- When I'm less stressed.
- When I've more money in the bank.
- When the mortgage is paid off.

I came to realise that I was looking too far ahead at the 'ideal finished life' and not at the next week, the next day or even the next moment. And yet all it took was me taking one step in the direction in which I wanted to go. Take a look at this simple exercise. Ask yourself these two questions:

- Can I take that step today?
- (And if not) what would I have to do first?

A seemingly unattainable, long-way-off 'goal' suddenly comes within reach. A long-way-off goal need not be done in a day. Isn't it exhilarating committing to taking that first step? The motion is energising. One step leads to another, sometimes we need to stop over-thinking and just take the next step and the next . . .

- *What do* you *want to do now, that you'll commit to in order to live the life you want?*

LESSON 31

Ask for help

Superheroes live in comic books and films, not in real life. It took me a long time to realise that asking for help wasn't a sign of weakness. Have *you* learned this lesson yet? We do not live in isolation – we are social animals and we all like to feel useful. But sometimes we need help from others. We might need to talk through our problems, ask for assistance with the housework, seek administrative support at work, or get help with our children.

There are no special prizes for worn-out would-be super-heroines.

Asking for help = a sign of weakness. That's what I used to believe. I wore myself into the ground trying to be Wonderwoman. If I didn't collapse on the sofa at 9.00 p.m., exhausted, then I obviously hadn't worked hard enough during the day. The image of the strong, competent, independent woman that I so longed to portray was incapable of reaching out to ask for help even though she so desperately needed it. I was too proud, too scared, too much in need of control to ask for help. It was, however, a lonely place to be, this not-so-splendid isolation of mine. But I came to understand that stoicism is overrated and I learned the value of saying, 'I could do with a hand here, please.'

I've learned to delegate and know that it doesn't make me an incapable person. I've learned to ask for help with my housekeeping because my time is better used elsewhere. I asked for help when I was building a website – IT is not my forte, so why should I allow such frustration in my life when there are gifted people out there?

As I write this, my son is cutting the grass and my daughter is preparing our next meal.

* *Where are* you *too hard on yourself?*

LESSON 32

Get red in your life

Red is the colour associated with passion, strength, energy, danger, courage, power, desire, and love. How about bringing some of this colour into your life? Lipstick, handbag, lingerie (tasteful, please), front door, feature wall in your bedroom, kettle, or toaster.

What is it about the colour red that excites me? It feels daring and racy. It feels energetic and vibrant and full of life.

I love how I feel when I wear my red shoes – both sneakers and heels. My red handbag always get noticed. I love looking at my red toenails. I have a red linen summer dress and I feel alive when I wear it. Red makes me feel invincible.

The first thing I did when it was just the children and me in the house was to repaint the front door from white to red. Everyone noticed (obviously) and remarked at how totally different it felt coming into the house. I smiled and relaxed as I approached my front door and that was a very good and satisfying feeling.

A friend painted her kitchen wall a deep red and suddenly the energy in the kitchen was electric – was it odd or natural that conversations became livelier, laughter became louder?

- *Where will you feature red in* your *life?*

LESSON 33

Celebrate your femininity

Wear a skirt or dress more often. Wear heels. (They needn't be your killer heels – even a little heel gives you a lift.) Did you know research suggests that wearing heels improves your sex life? Give your underwear drawer an overhaul. Get fitted for a bra. (Did you know that the majority of women wear the wrong size bra?) Wearing a bra that fits correctly gives us back our curves; we stand taller, feel better, and look sensational. Oh, and please: Best Knickers Always! There is no excuse for shabby knickers, ladies, whatever your budget.

Femininity means something different to all of us. I'm not a high-heeled girl, I'm much more comfortable in a pair of Converse, ballet pumps or flip-flops. Yet when I do wear heels, I feel sexy and for me that can often mean more feminine. It's got something to do with the angle we have to stand to remain upright. Since the time my girlfriend sent me the text reminding me to look after myself and to remember my best knickers always, I have vowed to do just that and always wear beautiful lingerie. I make sure that I am fitted for a bra regularly because all of these details allow me to feel feminine. I can then wear my ripped gardening jeans, boyfriend's sweatshirt – and still feel like Aphrodite. I love the power I feel in my femininity.

For me, femininity is about softness too; my son stroked my face after a particularly difficult patch and said that now everything was out in the open, I looked different, softer. Tenderness, nurturing, creativity, intuition, gentleness, kindness, are all feminine qualities if skirts and heels and lipstick aren't your kinda thing.

I've learned that, although I love how feminine I feel when I'm in my finest bra and knickers, femininity comes from within; it is who I am, how I think, how I feel and how I act that makes me feminine and not what I'm wearing.

- *How comfortable are* you *in your femininity?*

LESSON 34

Acceptance

Acceptance allows us to move on from the hurts of the past. Acceptance is empowering. It allows us to forgive ourselves and others and take charge of our lives. Acceptance allows us to begin to make positive changes. We are no longer held back by the past, by our anger, regret, resentment and sadness. Acceptance allows us to make clear-headed choices. Acceptance frees us to act with greater integrity and steers us in the direction in which we want to go. Let go of the past; live in the present.

I knew that if I wanted to move forward in life, I had to be willing to let go of what was holding me back. I stayed back if I failed to accept my current situation.

> God, give us grace to accept with serenity
> the things that cannot be changed,
> courage to change the things
> which should be changed,
> and the wisdom to distinguish
> the one from the other.

So wrote Reinhold Niebuhr, the American theologian. My grandmother had this prayer on a ceramic tile propped up on the windowsill on her landing. I would pass it and read it every time I headed to the bathroom in her home. As a young child I read it, yet never understood or, in fact, gave it much thought.

It's funny how, years later, it's one of the quotes I printed off and stuck to my fridge as a daily reminder for a little subliminal learning when things were tough. I had to learn serenity as there were many things I was struggling to accept, things that I would rant and rage about, things that were way beyond my control and, as a control freak at the time, this was a big one to learn. But learn serenity I did.

So how about accepting where we are in midlife? In not accepting a situation we give power to it. What is more powerful: to rage against the loss of a job or a relationship day in, day out, letting it consume our every waking hour, or accept that we've lost our job or our partner has left and use that to springboard us forwards?

How much energy was I wasting focusing on the things I could not change? It was leading to a sense of hopelessness, powerlessness and stress that had begun to show up physically in my body. Acceptance brings freedom. Acceptance allows us to make choices for our life. It will allow us to act with integrity and steer us forwards in the direction we want to go.

- *How is the past holding* you *back?*

LESSON 35

Clarity

Develop a clear vision of what you want for your life. The very first question my coach asked me was, 'What do you want?' The easy bit was knowing what I didn't want. What I *didn't* want, I felt with every fibre of my being. But what about what I wanted? I'd never given that much thought. Write down your dreams and your goals. Do not become attached to the outcome, yet work every day on something that will move you closer to what you want in your life – whether that's a new job or a better relationship.

Being clear about what I wanted began with having crystal-clear clarity about what I no longer wanted. I didn't want to feel the way I was feeling any longer. I didn't want to feel fearful. I didn't want to feel like the shadow of the woman I had once been. I didn't want to feel half awake. I didn't want to feel powerless any more. And I was absolutely fed up with feeling so timid. I was not born that way and those friends I made at university knew me as a fearless young woman. I had to get absolutely clear about what I wanted in my life.

I learned to have, and continue to have, unshakeable clarity in how I wanted my life to be. I created clarity in my thinking for the home I wanted for my children and myself.

I gained clarity for the type of relationship I wanted. I created clarity in the type of work I wanted to be doing and did everything I could (and I've done and continue to do all sorts of different jobs) to make sure there was food on the table for myself and my children.

- *With a bit of clarity what could you create for* your *life?*

LESSON 36

Responsibility

Stop blaming your parents, your boss, your ex, or your partner. Know that you and you alone are responsible for your life. This is a tough message, I know that. But taking full responsibility will liberate you. It will put you in charge of your life – and lessen the impact of others' actions on your course. Where do I now need to take full responsibility? It is a question I continue to ask myself regularly.

This was a big lesson for me and it's a tough one but, once mastered, it is joyously liberating for yourself and those around you. To take responsibility fully in every area of my life meant that there was no hiding place and no one to hide behind and blame for the situation. I've come to realise that not many people do it. Some people don't want to take responsibility for their health, their happiness, their work, their relationships. Some people just want someone to blame: life might be miserable but at least *they* don't have to take responsibility. I remember being in the school playground when my son was young. It was autumn and the leaves were pouring off the trees and I stood in utter disbelief as one mother screamed at the school caretaker that he was responsible for her son falling over and grazing his knees – in her eyes it was the caretaker's fault that her son had fallen over.

I took responsibility for *my* life. I wanted to be happy and it is nobody else's duty to make me happy: it must come from within. I needed to take on the responsibility to end my marriage and pay the potential price – the fallout, including the damage it might have done to my children – and the reaction from all those around me. I had to let go of judging myself in order to take responsibility.

- *What conversation would it be helpful to have with* yourself *today?*

LESSON 37

Make time for celebration

Most of us neglect celebration and some reserve only the most special of occasions for it. When you've had a good day, when things are going your way, wouldn't it be lovely to mark the moment by stopping for some act of celebration? Reward yourself for tiny achievements, especially during tough times. Give yourself a high-five in a way that suits you. And even those low days, the days where we've felt pretty dreadful, let us not neglect to celebrate that we did, in fact, make it to the end of the day. How will *you* celebrate? A few squares of your favourite chocolate? An overdue phone call with a friend overseas? A pizza out with the family? A long, candlelit soak in the bath? A manicure?

It's not something I was ever very good at. Perhaps it's an old, drummed-in work ethic about having to be productive at all times. Work, work, work until I collapsed into bed at night. Joy? What was that? I was missing something. Surely celebrating small successes was simply the manifestation of gratitude which I was so very good and deliberate about?

If I had the choice to say to a friend who was over from the US, 'I'd love to meet up' or 'I've got a ton of stuff that needs to be done, deadline, laundry, washing my hair . . .' I chose to meet up. All the other stuff would get done – we had to celebrate; it was one little victory and it had to be celebrated.

I celebrate the little things now, a cup of tea and a piece of cake in the garden when a small section of work has been completed, a smart new face product for achieving small goals in the gym, a high-five to myself for sticking with my daily meditation when it would be so easy to not find the time.

- *What deserves celebrating in* your *life?*

LESSON 38

It's okay to be vulnerable

Honestly, this is the one that has taken me the longest time to learn – and there are still plenty of days when I struggle with the fear of revealing my own vulnerability. We don't need to be the strong, mask-wearing superhero all the time. Showing our vulnerability gives those around us the chance to love us, to care for us. By letting go of an all-capable façade, we show trust and faith in other.

I am able to say today that I am a little more at ease with showing my vulnerability. It was not always so. Vulnerability to me was a sign of weakness. I needed to be strong and feisty and all-powerful and it was, of course, simply an illusion. Inside I was a little girl with scuffed shoes sitting on a swing with tears pricking her eyes, a little girl who just wanted to be loved. I love unconditionally, yet have always struggled with accepting unconditional love, believing I needed to be good to be loved. As I grew up, I felt unworthy of love: I wasn't good enough, or clever enough, or pretty enough.

It took a very special relationship for me to learn that I was safe to show my scars, to show my 'ugly' side, to cry and still be loved. I wasn't going to be abandoned because I felt vulnerable and 'weak'. In fact, I have come to realise and aim to show my clients that being vulnerable is an extraordinary act of courage. The original meaning of the word courage comes from the Latin 'cor' which means heart. So courage for me means living and feeling our way with our hearts . . . is this not what vulnerability is? Being courageous enough to say 'I love you', or 'I need help'?

- *How easy is it for* you *to reveal your vulnerability?*

LESSON 39

Spend time in the company of real beauty

Beauty uplifts the soul at all times. I love spending time in art galleries and exhibitions, learning to appreciate the gift, the effort, and the time that goes into creating art. I cherish my time with 'beautiful' people – those who radiate goodness and love. And I am restored by the time I spend in nature, taking wild and windy beach walks or wandering in green and tranquil pastures or the ancient woods near my home.

When I was at my most overwhelmed, I would put on

my walking boots, grab the dog and head to the woods. My heart and my soul are calmed when I'm in the woods, whatever the season and whatever the weather. The woods are untamed and this inspires me. I feel safe and protected there. The trees are ancient and the undergrowth is fragrant and green. Nature is real beauty for me. The woods are my spiritual home. Trees that raise up towards the heavens and have their roots very firmly deep in the ground – their majesty encourages me to bravery and strengthens me.

Whenever I return to the place I grew up, I walk the cliff path from one beach to another. It refreshes me and inspires me and uplifts me – nature in all its splendid beauty. There is such beauty in wilderness. I would return from my walk rebalanced, reconnected with myself, life a little more in perspective.

- *What beauty uplifts your soul?*

LESSON 40

Have a hero and a mentor

A mentor and role model need not be someone you know personally: for that matter, he or she might not even be alive. Whose writing inspires you? Whose work excites you? Who do you admire? Who do you respect and look up to? Dedicate time to learning from that person.

I still miss my grandfather, the wisest man I have ever known. He was my hero and my mentor, the man I turned to when I doubted the big things in life. He was an adoring and an adored grandfather and great-grandfather. He was a man ahead of his time, erudite, interested in life and living right up until he died in his nineties, his mind as sharp as a tack. He is one of my guardian angels and I wish he had been around to listen and advise when things became really tough in my life. As a writer himself, he'd have been so proud of what his granddaughter is achieving, that she battled with her own demons and was brave enough to listen to her own counsel. The timid soul that I felt myself to be at times was not the girl he would have described, of that I am certain.

Although a devout Catholic, he was open-minded enough to embrace all faiths. He taught me non-judgment. He taught me tolerance. He taught me to do what I felt deep inside to be right. He taught me determination and bloody-mindedness. I think about him often and ask myself when in doubt, 'What would Pa say?'

- *What questions would you ask your mentor or hero?*

LESSON 41

Tackle a fear head-on

There was a time when anything official that came through my front door was left in a pile on the kitchen table. I felt physically sick when I thought of looking at my bank statement. Personal finance was my Achilles heel and I was completely fearful. And then it had to change because, as a single parent, I *needed* to take active responsibility for my finances. Now I open my mail, check my finances online, and work out how much money I actually have. I know my monthly expenditure and fixed outgoings – and my life is less stressful as a result.

I had to get a grasp of my finances very quickly and find creative ways to make money, so I couldn't afford to be financially illiterate any longer. Financial independence was what I needed as soon as I divorced, I needed to rely on myself. I had always been terrified of money, fearful of never having enough, full of old, deep-rooted fears of not having enough of anything. Being financially dependent on someone else was not conducive to having a positive attitude around money. I grew up thinking that money was always scarce, that others could have it but not me.

A friend created a spreadsheet for me – a spreadsheet! That in itself filled me with terror. I was to input all my fixed outgoings – utilities, mobiles, debt repayment, rent, and list all my income from all sources. This then left me with a 'daily allowance' for food and everything else. It was sobering, but at least now I was in charge and it felt liberating: I was empowered. And you know what? I did it; I managed my finances. There is something remarkably liberating in getting a grip on this stuff and I removed the fear by facing it full on, by opening the letters and looking at my bank balance. It's amazing what you can achieve when the alternative is oh so much worse.

- *How different would* you *feel if you tackled a fear head-on?*

LESSON 42

Cultivate friendships

Women need girlfriends. We thrive with our friends. We share, we support, we love, we give. I have an annual Girl-friends' Dinner where my close friends and I express our gratitude for each other. There is laughter, and there are tears. I know that my journey these past years has been made bearable because of the unconditional support of my 'tribe'.

This is the letter I sent out to my girlfriends inviting them to my most recent Girls' Night In.

The last few years have been one hell of a roller coaster for me. I've often been left wondering how on earth I managed to board this particular fairground attraction. So much has happened in the last five years that, at times, I've been on the verge of losing the plot entirely and, if it hadn't been for you, my beloved friends, who knows what kind of basket-case I'd be right now. Some of you I've known all my life and some more recently. All of you have supported me in one way or another on this journey.

I want to celebrate the end of an era and the beginning of an awfully big adventure. When one door closes, a thousand others open to greet us. I'd love to get you all together for a Girls' Night In to thank you all for your love, kindness, kicks up the bum, tissues, encouragement, long-distance phone calls, alcohol and coffee.

We were a group of women coming together, some knowing each other and others meeting for the first time. I was the common denominator. We ate, we drank, we laughed, we cried and we told stories of our lives and our experiences. Some single, some married, some widowed, some with children and others without, some working full time, others full-time mums. All happy to learn about and from each other. All richer for this real exchange.

- *Who are the friends you could call on at 3.00 a.m.?*

LESSON 43

Look after yourself

Treat yourself with respect. Eat well, exercise, learn to love yourself as you love others, get enough sleep, drink water, edit your wardrobe and wear SPF15 cream every day. Take a look at your addictions and all that you do to self-sabotage – food, alcohol, tobacco, negative self-talk. Isn't it time to turn to your inner healer for support?

How were you raised? Were you raised to believe that looking after your needs was selfish? That it was more important to put the needs of others above your own? Remember from the introduction how the name Best Knickers Always came about? I wasn't looking after myself.

I was sitting on the airplane, half listening whilst the stewards ran through the security instructions, you know the one – nearest exit, taking heels off so you don't puncture the inflatable slide, life jackets under the seat – and then it hit me right between the eyes 'oxygen masks will automatically fall from the ceiling in the event of a reduction in cabin pressure, make sure you fit your own mask before you help anyone else'. Obvious, isn't it? Yet this was not how I was living my life. I was racing around putting everyone else's oxygen masks on before putting on my own. How was I going to make sure that my body had good-quality oxygen pumping around my body? What did I need to do to look after myself?

• *How are* you *going to look after yourself?*

LESSON 44

Surprise yourself and your friends

I like this: it's playful and there's a lot to be said for having more fun and playfulness in our lives. What could you do that's a little different and out of character? Well, stretch yourself in a fun way. Surprise yourself. How about learning a musical instrument or learning to dance? Which appeals to you? Piano or cello? Samba or ballroom? Meet new people by supporting a local society? Volunteer for something you're passionate about?

Me, I've just had purple highlights put in my silver hair. It was a surprise for me and it certainly has been for my friends and family. I love people's reactions: some adore it, some not so much. And some clearly enjoy living vicariously, knowing they'd never do it themselves!

A friend travelled alone from the USA to London to spend a week writing and sightseeing – some friends were worried for her safety, others were thrilled at her sense of adventure.

I dated younger men and had a lot of fun. It surprised some friends and shocked others. A forensic scientist friend went on a cake-decorating course – that's very different for her. A friend's husband amazed me when he told me that he used to be a professional saxophonist . . . his day job is as a lawyer. Now *that's* cool. And I have an ultra-cool friend who works in advertising. He wants nothing more than to be a gardener because he is at his happiest when his hands are in compost.

And I have still not ruled out a tattoo.

Think of this as an alternative bucket list.

- *What would* you *like to do?*

LESSON 45

Nourish your spirit

We are spiritual beings and would do well to nourish this part of ourselves. I find enormous benefit from my daily meditation practice. Some find their nourishment in prayer and churchgoing; others find it through walks in the woods. Find what heals and replenishes your soul. Doing good work, practising random acts of kindness, meditating, and chanting can all work to nourish our souls.

I have a chattering-monkey mind. If I wake in the night, I have to be very still and pretend not to have woken in an attempt to keep the monkey in my head asleep. Meditation is something I had hoped to be good at: I imagined myself all Zen-like, sitting crossed-legged on my cushion, getting myself to an enlightened state . . . Nope. What I do find, though, is that I am a calmer, more alert, more relaxed, more thoughtful and purposeful person because of my daily meditation practice. I have learned, through guided meditation, not to judge the monkey mind, just to observe and let thoughts come in and out, to sit on the sidelines and observe thoughts rather than engage in them. It takes practice. Daily practice.

Meditation nourishes me. I am more mindful because of it and I have learned that there is no competition in meditation: we practice meditation and it is neither good nor bad. It simply is.

- *What are the daily practices that nourish* your *spirit?*

LESSON 46

Learn from those older and younger than you

I am blessed with friends spanning many decades. I miss my dear old neighbour who died from cancer because we spent many hours talking of life and loves. I also revel in being with the young: I delight in their spontaneity, their innocence, and 'anything is possible' outlook.

Don't be in a rush to judge — both the elderly and the young have wisdom to share.

When we are wading through mud, when our vision and perspective on our situation is so narrowed down and blinkered that it is very difficult to see outside of ourselves and our problems, this is the time to get a different perspective. This is when it is good to spend time with people outside of our age group. This is the time to sit on the floor playing Lego with a small child, the time to sit besides them as they are creating a masterpiece at their easel. These wise young souls have much to teach us if we turn down the background noise in our own heads and give these little people our full attention. Such wisdom, there, if we simply listen for it. They see things in their paintings that we can only dream of as we try to rationalise and make sense of the brush strokes on their paper.

Or perhaps it's sitting down with an elderly friend who is dying and talking about what the important things in life truly are. Approaching goodbyes mean we talk about the truth, love and where to focus our life and not on working harder or wanting the latest gadget or getting mad because someone cut us up at the lights.

I am always uplifted and renewed.

- *Who could show* you *a different perspective on life?*

LESSON 47

What is your deepest desire?

This is a big, important question. Our lives are short, and we need to know that they have meaning and purpose. Do not delay living a life that is less than authentically yours. What might your future self tell the 'you' of today?

My first coach asked me this question, 'What is your deepest desire?' Frankly, he might well have been speaking Chinese to me. I had no idea what he meant, but my subconscious mind did, of course, and was delighted. Back then, I could only come up with answers like – my deepest desire is to make it to bedtime, to sleep through the night, to hope that my children are happy today.

Meaning and purpose? What's that about, then? Of course I knew *exactly* what that was, but I was caught up in the pain of existing day-to-day. Deeply unhappy and unfulfilled, I was living a life on autopilot, a life that I was expected to live. Magazines are full of it – The Lifestyle. My coach asked, no, *told* me, to buy a beautiful journal and start writing . . . writing? I can't write, I said. He insisted. 'I want you to write, blind writing, either with the hand you don't usually write with or just write without judging, correcting or re-reading and editing.' Oh lord! But I obeyed and began to write. I began with the words, 'I'm writing because I've been told to write, that it will help unlock my thoughts . . .' and I wrote and I wrote and I wrote and I couldn't stop.

What were my deepest desires? Through tears I wrote them down and they had nothing to do with financial success, sports cars and luxury apartments by the seaside. I longed for peace, for contentment, for joy, for a life lived with purpose and for passion. Oh, I longed for passion. My words came into focus and I slowly and painfully found clarity.

* *What calls* you *deeply?*

LESSON 48

Believe in the goodness of humanity

Too many people live closed-off lives, believing someone is out to get them – or, worse, that it's better to 'get them before they get you'. And then there are the people who are always let down, always disappointed, by others. I firmly believe that if you have that mentality, then disappointment is exactly what you'll get. We all tend to get from life what we expect to get. I choose to expect to find goodness in humanity and to revel in the kindness of strangers. And you know what? Time and time again, I receive goodness and generosity from others.

I'm a glass-half-full kinda girl. Like most people, I'm sure, it wasn't always that way. During my years of depression I was anything but — I was an empty glass. But I'm back on track. These days I'm the kind of person who always finds parking spaces, always wins things, is always treated as I would want to be treated; I trust people and find that people trust me in return and I believe that things will always turn out okay. There are those who call this way of thinking naïve and New Age. Well, you know what? I don't care that I'm an optimist because there are more than enough pessimists and 'realists' out there and I find my optimistic outlook good for my health. I read something the other day that went a bit like this: the definition of an optimist is someone who knows that taking a step backward, after taking a step forward, is not the end of the world; it's more like a cha-cha.

I've learned to ask for and expect good things to come my way. I teach my children to do the same and we all find that people are more than willing to help and that people are extraordinarily generous with their time, their connections and their practical help.

- *How different would life be if you believed in the goodness of humanity?*

LESSON 49

Have no regrets

We all make mistakes; it's how we chart our course. Children learn from their mistakes as they move through childhood, and it's no different for us. Life is too short to live with regrets. Fast-forward to the end of your life and imagine you are looking back at where you are today. What will your thoughts be? Over and over, my answer has been to let go of guilt, because it only holds me back. Accept our mistakes. We're human – erring is what we do. Forgive yourself, and move on.

I've reached midlife, I've celebrated my fiftieth birthday, and I'm happy and deeply content and excited about not only now but my future. I believe being in midlife right now is an exciting place to be.

I could so easily look back over my life and regret many things – I could have trusted my own mind and intuition and forged a different path in my early twenties; I could have regretted the years of depression, the years of feeling inadequate; I could have realised that I was unhappy in my marriage earlier and done something about it years before. I could have, I should have, I ought to have . . . NO! No regrets. My life has shaped me into the woman I am today. I am who I am today because of my experiences.

How could I regret all that?

- *What would* you *like to let go of right this moment?*

LESSON 50

Be bodacious

Let us be bold and stand up for ourselves, let us be audacious and ask for what we want. 'Each of us has the right,
that possibility, to invent ourselves daily. If a person does
not invent herself, she will be invented. So, to be bodacious
enough to invent ourselves is wise,' says Maya Angelou,
a writer for whom I have huge admiration. Having led a
tough life, like so many black women of her generation,
she inspires me to greatness.

What if I believed I had that right, that possibility to
re-invent myself, I used to ask myself. What if I believed
I could leave my marriage which was making me desperately unhappy?

How can you afford to leave? I was asked. But I had
got to the place where the question I was asking was: how
can I afford to stay? Emotionally, I was a wreck. And yet
. . . there was this very strong, very brave, very bold and,
dare I say it, audacious women living in my body making
her voice louder and clearer each day. I no longer wanted
to be 'invented', I wanted to be the woman I knew I was

deep inside. I wanted to create my own life; I wanted to be bolder than I ever thought possible; I wanted to trust in my own wisdom, my own intuition. I wanted to inspire and give courage to other women to do the same, to embrace midlife, to celebrate where we'd got to, all we'd achieved at this point in our lives and to look forward to an exciting second half of our lives.

• *What would* you *do if you were ten times bolder?*

Midlife Issues

So let's take a look at the bigger picture, shall we? What does midlife mean to you? What are the issues that we are all facing as we come into the second half of our lives? How different are our lives as women in midlife today compared to those of our mothers and grandmothers?

Marianne Williamson, a favourite author of mine writes of midlife: 'How would we live were we not afraid of death? How would we live if we felt we had full permission from ourselves and others to give everything we've got to life? Would midlife be time to shut down, or time to finally get started? Would it be time to give up, or time to claim what we really want?' I certainly know where I stand – how about you? Maybe you are questioning your life for the very first time or maybe you've been feeling the need for change for quite a while. Or perhaps you've got your life exactly where and how you want it. Either way, I hope that reading this book helps you realise that you are not alone, that there are plenty of us accompanying you on your journey through midlife.

In this second half of the book I've written about the issues that many of us are facing; some are mine and some are those of friends and other midlife women I've spoken with. You'll get no long diatribe on the misery of ageing from me – there's plenty of that in the media. Just type 'Midlife' into Google and the first thing that comes up is 'Crisis'. If you've got this far in the book, you'll have realised by now that my midlife glass is half-full and filling up daily.

What I write about are the day-to-day things that touch us now that we are in our forties, fifties and sixties, and consider how we can embrace these issues rather than rage against them. How can we make our lives easier and more comfortable as we get older? How can we buck the trend that old = over the hill? What you'll find here are my views – certainly not a list of 'shoulds' and 'shouldn'ts' to make you feel inadequate. If these views support you or help you question where you are in life, then I am pleased. Each of us is different and your experiences and issues in midlife are likely to be different to mine.

Empty nest

Empty nest *syndrome*, no less. Although not a clinical condition, it is seen as an important issue and the cause of great distress for many women. Children leaving home can be devastating for some. Although we know right from birth that our children are only on loan to us, that they will and should leave home, it can come as a traumatic shock when it happens. Some of us grieve when our children leave and it raises a great many issues for us.

The greatest of these is: 'Who am I?' Our personal identity and sense of self often becomes lost in the 'we' of family life. As mothers we enjoy being needed, and as that role changes we find ourselves faced with a gaping void. If our career has been our children, then it can be deeply painful when they leave as there is, at that point, nothing to fill the gap.

- Who am I if I am no longer needed as a mother on a day-to-day basis?
- What is my purpose if not to mother?

Grieve if you need to – I did. We long to hear their voices, to smell them, to curl up on the sofa with them and, yes, even to argue with them, and there is an aching emptiness when this ends. My eldest left home at the same time as my marriage was coming to an end. I grieved for both these endings and, for a time, I was blinded and unable to see the opportunity for new beginnings; I was lost in no-man's land.

I have gone from three, to two, to one left in the nest, so mine is almost empty. I love my children dearly, but I also love my own life, my space, and my time alone with my new partner. Once we get over the pain of separation from our children we can enjoy what, for some, feels like a guilty pleasure . . . time spent away from them.

I love my nest when the children are not in it as much as I love it when they are – take a look at what my nest looks like when it's just me.

- The nest is tidy.
- There is food in the fridge.
- The toothpaste is squeezed correctly.
- Towels can be found in the bathroom drying on the towel rail and not on bedroom floors.
- The laundry basket doesn't go from empty to overflowing overnight.
- The kitchen sink is not loaded with dishes.
- Beds are made and curtains opened in the morning.
- Milk, cereal and bread last more than twenty-four hours.
- Glasses, mugs and cereal bowls are to be found in kitchen cupboards and not in various rooms, their insides looking like some biological experiments.
- The radio station plays *my* music.
- There are no bags and coats and size ten shoes at the bottom of the stairs to trip over.
- Sex doesn't have to be quite so impromptu and furtive and quiet.
- Lipstick, body lotion, razor and hair gel are where they'd been left.

I have loved every stage of my children's development; some have been frustrating and challenging, yet I've always known that it will pass, that nothing is forever. Leaving home can feel like the final stage as we wave them goodbye as they head off to university or help them move into their first flat. It is, however, simply just another stage in their development (and ours). We can welcome them back for family meals, for Christmas trips out together, for a visit to the cinema to see the film we've heard so much about, for a girls' day out shopping or a trip to the stadium to support our favourite team. And this time it can all can be done as two adults rather than as parent and child.

We'll always be 'Mum' and have words of wisdom or opinions to share and at this stage our children can choose to listen or not, to ask for advice or ask their friends. This is *their* life now, their journey and their path. We have given them both the roots to know home and the wings to fly.

Boomerang kids

'Boomerang kids' are a relatively new phenomenon. Given the current economic climate, and no doubt because there's central heating and a full fridge, and looking after yourself day in, day out as a student wasn't as exciting as first antici-pated, children often return to the nest after completing their studies. Usually, because incomes are very low for those starting out in work and accommodation and the cost of living is high, our young adults struggle to be independent on their income, so they return to the family home. And for those who didn't leave at eighteen to head off to continue in education, many are remaining at home until well into their twenties. Both these situations bring their own issues that must be tackled as a family. Communication and open dialogue, adult to adult, becomes vital at this stage. How can we create a workable balance; giving them the opportunity to become free-thinking adults, to make choices for their lives whilst we continue family living, expecting them to abide by our rules and respect our values? Different rules need to be applied and a new set of boundaries needs to be put in place if we are to 'enjoy' our adult children back at home.

It's not easy. We've got used to them being away, got used to our ways of doing things, of peace perhaps, of a certain level of neatness to our lives. Suddenly all that changes. We can no longer treat them like the 'children' they were before they left. Yet, in return, they cannot treat home as they perhaps treated their university house.

Tensions can arise when there is no communication. Our children do not read our minds so ask them, remind them of their responsibility in family living. Let them know that if they want to be treated as an adult then they too must behave as an adult behaves. It might seem like tough love, but they are now living in our home as an adult and no longer as a child under our care. Unless we want thirty-year-old children in our nest, then we must take action from the outset and not make life too easy and comfortable for them.

Boundaries and rules are key. Chores and a contribution to the family budget is something to be discussed. Yes, they are our children, but we don't want them freeloading if we are to teach them about budgeting and living in an adult world now they are in their twenties. I love my children dearly, yet also want to teach them about self-responsibility. One of mine was back home for nine months before leaving again – and we were both happy with this arrangement.

(Anti)-ageing

Let me begin by saying that I have a problem with the term anti-ageing. We age. That's life. Why should we be anti ageing if it is, after all, what we all do? Let's instead embrace ageing. Let's be role models for the younger generation. We have to fight hard enough as it is, without hating our own bodies for doing what they do naturally. Yes, gravity is active in my body – my breasts and cheeks aren't where they used to be, I am slim but my stomach most definitely shows that I carried three children.

The issue for me is the media's obsession with the Holy Grail that is 'youth'. We see it daily in touched-up photos of celebrities advertising another wonder cream or magnification, in signs of ageing in the same celebrities. How does that affect us mere mortals? It means we spend a ridiculous amount on anti-ageing products – and at the same time we feel disillusioned and dissatisfied at best, and depressed at worst, with our own ageing bodies.

I have no problem with those of us who choose to plump up or boost or enhance our faces and bodies in order to feel good about ourselves. My thoughts, and those of friends I've spoken with on surgery and needles, are simple: know absolutely why you want to do it. Don't have surgery to make changes to your body if you are hoping to mask your low self-esteem. Surgery is not some magic wand that takes all your troubles away. It's like saying that having a baby will save a failing marriage. If you have low self-esteem, take a look at the causes of it before you consider surgery. Get some sense of how you view yourself when you look in the mirror. Are you self-critical and judgmental? Having a tummy tuck or losing a chin is unlikely to alter that critical voice.

I had a vial of hyaluronic acid (dermal filler) injected into my face at a point in my life where I knew I didn't look my age. I was forty-eight and knew I looked old and tired and haggard. I knew this to be true because friends would tell me I looked exhausted and worn-out (love the honesty of friends, don't you?). The result was that as I looked old and haggard, so I felt it and it became a downward spiral. I knew that if I looked in the mirror and saw a woman whose face was less drawn, then I would feel brighter and more vibrant.

I told my doctor that I didn't want my wrinkles and lines to disappear. I simply wanted to look my age again. And I did. No one knew or commented, apart from telling me that I looked well and rested. And that's exactly how I came to feel. Well and rested and ready for anything.

We must, however, let go of the need to still look twenty when we see ourselves in the mirror. I have lines, wrinkles around my eyes and around my mouth, my skin is not as plump and elastic as it was – you just need to use one of those horrific hand-driers to see the reduction in elastin in practice. Yet my wisdom, my ease with myself is, for me, a price well worth paying. I would not trade these for tighter skin.

My question is, I guess: 'Who do you see when you look in the mirror?' Do you see an old, lined, ageing woman who misses the girl she once was? Or do you see an older woman who loves who she sees, her lines telling the story of her life so far, her experiences and her wisdom which have been hard earned? Ask yourself which you see. If you are unhappy with who you see, ask yourself what are you missing from your youth, what do you long for from that period of your life? What is it you fear?

Do you want to know the best (anti)-ageing products? Happiness and fulfilment. And those, my friends, money cannot buy. Oh, and a good regular haircut if you really must spend some money. I recently bumped into a friend I hadn't seen for perhaps four years and, after chatting for a while, she stopped me and asked, 'How do you do it? You look younger, your skin, your eyes – you look vibrant!' My response was, 'I'm happy and fulfilled in my life.'

Relationships and standing the test of time

Helen Fielding's much loved character Bridget Jones refers to those in relationships as the 'Smug Marrieds' and, having spoken with a bunch of friends on 'How to Keep a Long-Term Relationship Alive and Well' and 'How Come Yours Stood the Test of Time and Mine Didn't?', I can assure you that these couples are anything but smug. There is no room for complacency when it comes to long marriages and part-nerships. These relationships work because those involved work at it. They prioritise and place great emphasis on their 'couple'.

So how do you sit down to dinner opposite someone you may well have been with for well over two decades and know that you still love them and look forward to growing old with them? I spoke with men and women for this section and it inspires me as I look forward to my future and a long-lasting relationship.

In no particular order, here are some non-negotiables for a long and happy relationship:

- **Friendship:** to actually like and be friends with your partner is the very foundation. It sounds obvious, but it's often where marriages start to fall apart; when we not only stop loving someone but actually start to dislike them. Best Friends Forever.

- **Sense of humour:** lots of laughing together. Seeing the funny side to life, not taking oneself too seriously, being able to laugh at ourselves and be teased. These are vital.

- **Communication:** is the key to a successful relationship. Remember that your spouse is not a mind-reader, even though you've been married for twenty-five years. Ask for what you want, talk about what's bothering you and never go to sleep on an argument or disagreement. We do become more set in our ways as we get older, but give up on trying to change your partner. Love them as they are, accept things, discuss what you believe matters to you and decide what's really important.

- **Our time:** book time in the diary to do things together, even if it's just walking the dog, having a bike ride, or going to the cinema at least once a month. It's vital and it doesn't need to be expensive. Cook a lovely meal at home, tell the kids this is mum and dad time and sit and talk (no TV allowed).

- **Sex:** yes, it's important and yes, it gets better as we get older. Be prepared to be spontaneous in your sex life. Living with small children, teenagers and boomerang kids is not conducive to easy bedtime sex, so grab it when you can. Book a night away a couple of times a year or arrange sleepovers for your children so you can have the house to yourselves for the night. It's so easy to slip into the habit of not having sex and it's not difficult to come up with all sorts of excuses. Be playful, flirt, keep that fire burning – remember back to the time you first met.

- **Space for each other:** having your own interests and friends makes for a strong relationship. Allow the other to do the things they love to do. That may well mean being happy whilst one watches sport all weekend so do your own thing, get on with your own stuff. Show interest in what your spouse loves to do without necessarily getting involved. Take one couple I know: he's a passionate cyclist and she's a whatever-the-weather golfer. They show interest in each other's sport yet feel no need to take it up. They appreciate their differences. A claustrophobic relationship is asking for trouble. Trust and understanding make for a healthy relationship.

- **Childproof the relationship:** we love our children very much, this goes without saying; yet one day they leave the nest and you're left with one another. Successful, respectful marriages seem to be those where the couple comes first. This is not about neglecting the children – it is more about valuing and treasuring the relationship that created the children. Kiss your spouse first, hug them and cuddle them, let the children see the importance of the relationship. Never be afraid of closing the bedroom door. When you come in from work and your spouse and children are already at home, speak with your spouse first – the children's demands and clamouring (especially if they are little) can surely wait five minutes.

Divorce and moving on

Divorce sucks. Whether instigated by ourselves or coming at us like an express train, it hurts us to our core. The pain is visceral in its intensity. When we made our till-death-do-us-part vows, we meant it. And then life happens whilst we're busy and we change and/or grow – and unless we work hard and communicate and *both* put great value on our marriage, then these changes become the things we fight over. Strong and lasting marriages take work – they just don't happen by themselves. Are there more demands on us than on our parents and grandparents generation? Is it simply easier and less of a stigma to become part of the divorce statistics than it was?

Interestingly, current statistics show a fall in the divorce rate, apart from the over-sixties where 'silver separation' is on the rise. There are myriad reasons for divorce, but with divorce later in life it's usually because we come to realise that the person we married is no longer our mate, our friend, or someone we want to grow old with. The children have left or are leaving home and we don't want to put up with loneliness in a loveless marriage any longer. We would rather go it alone. We are no longer staying together for the children.

So how do we move on from divorce? How do we start again? How do you get used to being single and independent again?

I'd say by taking it easy, one day at a time; in fact, one *moment* at a time some days. There will be days when the tears either won't stop or won't come. There will be days where everything is black. There will also be days when we find we have made a simple step forward. Celebrate this achievement. Let go of judging the bad days and be grateful for the good moments. Time heals everything: it may sound trite but it is true. Give yourself time to grieve. Get help from a professional to talk through your emotions – friends and family can be supportive, but they do come with their own agenda.

As I was working through my own divorce, I spent a lot of time writing about my feelings and sharing my deepest emotions in my journal. It was cathartic, it was liberating, and it was healing. I came to believe that there are five essential stages that enable us to move on from a negative and helpless place to one where we feel enabled and peaceful: Acceptance, Courage, Clarity, Non-Judgment and Personal Responsibility. I have written about each of these earlier in the book as part of the Fifty Lessons; however I would also like to add the following thoughts because these five stages are all equally important and work together in freeing us.

- **Acceptance** allows us to forgive: to forgive ourselves for whatever part we might have played in the breakdown of the marriage, to forgive ourselves for our behaviour which at times may have been manipulative and underhand. Acceptance over time allows us to forgive our ex for their role and behaviour in the divorce too. Acceptance allows us to forgive the past and move forward with grace and a good conscience.

- Acceptance brings **responsibility,** a responsibility for our
  life and ourselves. Taking full responsibility for our life
  requires honesty from us. We have to suck up the bad
  stuff and we get to celebrate fully in the good stuff. The
  buck stops with us when we are responsible for our life.
  We make much more enlightened choices when we know
  that we can't fall back and blame someone else when
  things don't turn out quite right. We think more carefully
  about the outcomes when we are steering our own ship.

- Acceptance also requires **non-judgment** of ourselves and
  of others. I read once that it only takes one person to act
  with integrity during a divorce, so make sure that person
  is you. Divorce is a highly stressful time for those going
  through it; if we heap self-judgment on top, we simply
  crank up the stress levels. It is difficult not to judge ourselves and those on the other side of the table at this time
  but it is never, ever useful. We lash out or become defensive when we feel threatened, so let go of judging how
  you're behaving and feeling and work instead on being
  kind and forgiving towards yourself. Lighten up a little on
  yourself, allow yourself to be imperfect and, at the same
  time, remember (even if just for a moment) that the other
  person in this divorce is also not behaving at their best
  because they too feel threatened.

- Acceptance requires us to be courageous and often this might feel like stepping out into the great unknown. Trust that you can do what you need to do because we do find strength when we trust and the road does appear before us the minute we find the **courage** to take the first step. You are no doubt surrounded by those who love you – call on them to hold your hand.

- **Clarity** comes once we let go of blame – blame clouds our vision because we are letting responsibility for our own lives rest with someone else. Decide what you want for your own life; become clear in your thinking and your vision. Blame blinds us, filling us with resentment, anger and sadness. Let it go.

The dating game

Unless you've been asleep, had your head in the sand or are happily married, you'll know that more and more women are turning to the Internet to meet a new partner in later life. Several years back I was certain I'd meet a partner the 'old-fashioned' way, through a friend. Well, that wasn't to be because dinner party dates became fewer and further between. Was a single, lively, midlife woman a bit of a liability? Was I seen as a threat by the women, who didn't want me 'flirting' with their men? Was I far too free and happy and unattached for the guys who feared me 'putting ideas' in their wives' heads (true story)? So online dating it had to be.

Online dating is not for the faint-hearted. I had one friend who created a spreadsheet of different sites she was registered on, what dates she went on and the number of 'hits' on her profile. She was fairly clinical about the whole process, seeing it as a numbers game, but my attitude was not so clinical. For a start, I hate spreadsheets and am much more laissez faire. But, at the same time, some sort of plan is advisable.

What would I suggest? Here are my rules of engagement:

- Take nothing personally.
- See it as fun.
- Have the right positive attitude before spending your time on dating websites.
- Expect to giggle at some of the people who want to get in touch with you.
- Be business-like about it. I see it as modern day match-making. You get to email and phone before meeting. Life and free time is precious, so it's important to get to know the person beforehand.
- Enjoy yourself.
- Don't go into it imagining that you'll find your lifelong partner immediately.

- Decide what you want to get out of online dating. The first site I joined was for fun. I was looking for a bit of confidence-boosting and excitement and that's what I got – at that stage I wasn't looking for a serious, long-term relationship; I wanted to explore a bit.
- Be truthful and expect the same in return.
- Ask lots of questions, from the light-hearted to the more penetrating.
- Know what's important to you.
- Be committed to the process.
- Don't get disillusioned after a couple of dud dates.
- Write a compelling profile – write something different. A great profile is vital. Get some help in doing so if you're not that confident.
- Invest in some excellent photographs.
- Be open-minded.
- Be sensible and safe. Let a friend know where you are going and what time you expect to be home. Text her to let her know you're safe.
- Take your car on your date: it will mean that you'll watch what you drink.

More sex please

There is much written about the drop in libido that supposedly takes place in midlife. My view is that it's an excuse.

Ask yourself these important questions:

- Am I using this as an excuse because I can't be bothered to make the effort to have sex?
- Do I want to have sex with my partner?

Sex is an important part of a relationship and like everything to do with relationships it takes communication and practice. There is so much more to sex than penetration, as we all know. I'm no Dr Ruth, but do feel that most issues can be dealt with if discussed, and if talking about sex with your partner is something you've never done, then why not start today? There are plenty of products on the market to relax us and to lubricate us, so please don't use that as your reason for not having sex.

If sex is something that totally disinterests you, then so be it. Remember, however, the benefits of an active sex life. Sex can become so much more fulfilling as we get older. We don't worry about fertility. We are (usually) more confident. As with most things, the more you practice the better you become (yes, our children would be horrified to hear that). We've ditched performance anxiety. Frankly, we have nothing to prove.

NB: For those embarking on new relationships in midlife . . . there is a startling rise in STIs in the over-fifties. We grew up as the pill generation and our early sexual experiences were pre-Aids, a time when many of us didn't use condoms. Sadly, this cavalier attitude is no longer acceptable. Do not take the risk. And, ladies, do not have sex with that man if he's not prepared to use a condom. If you are embarking on something longer-term, then make sure you both get to the local sexual health clinic for a check-up. You'll be amazed at the variety of ages and backgrounds of people taking responsibility for their own sexual health.

Mental health

Our self-esteem can take quite a battering at various stages in our lives and I know from experience that midlife can be one of those occasions. Midlife brings us to a crossroads; it's one of those major transitions in life. Our roles are changing, whether we have had children or not, and we often question who we are. Some of us begin to question our validity and our purpose in life. We can look in the mirror and feel disheartened at the ageing woman we see. We miss and long for the woman who once had a vibrant complexion, plump skin and bright eyes, the woman who was excited about her future, her goals and dreams.

Mental health is a big topic and one that I could not hope to do justice to within the confines of this book. It is, however, a subject that is still shrouded in shame. We don't often talk about it, or our feelings, or our fears. I remember my grandmother teaching me that 'a problem shared is a problem halved' and to a degree I believe she was right. Talking through my feelings and my issues was invaluable. Speaking with a professional therapist who helped me make sense of where I was in my life and why I was feeling these things helped me enormously and now I live my life in a much more positive way.

Depression, along with agoraphobia and panic attacks, affect many of us. We can so often experience loneliness and isolation as our children don't need us as much, we may well have let hobbies slip in the busyness of life, and some of us have questions about the emptiness in our relationships. We can become introverted in our thinking and shut down in order to protect ourselves. I know this, I became like this. People believed me to be aloof and diffident; in truth, I was only just holding it together and I wore sunglasses whatever the weather in order to hide from friends' questioning. Do not ignore these issues. Finding someone to talk to can so easily help us to make sense of where we are and what we want for the second half of our lives. You will find that you are not alone. I have suffered with periods of depression throughout my adult life and, more recently, panic attacks. I sought help. Now I am well, the odd down day will no longer send me over the edge. It takes courage to confront an issue that we fear, but I do urge you to speak to someone – your GP or a close friend would make a great start.

Illness

I know from talking with those around me that serious illness is one of our greatest fears in midlife. Not a week goes by without learning about some new diagnosis someone we know has been given. We are all being touched by illness we ourselves have contracted, or we have nursed someone, or know someone in our close circle who has and is undergoing treatment of one sort or another. We are mortal beings and it is often at this time of life that we get a great big reminder of the fact that life is short. Now more than ever we must take responsibility for our health. Now is the time to be vigilant and to encourage friends to be so too. Act on any worries you have: that lump you keep feeling in the shower, that feeling of fatigue however much sleep you are getting, that change in a mole on your leg that you keep thinking about, that cough your dad has that doesn't seem to go away. All these must be checked out with your GP. Burying our heads in the sand is no way to live.

We must eat well and exercise regularly, protecting our bodies from illness in every way we can. Now is absolutely the time to stop smoking, reduce our alcohol intake and maintain a healthy weight. Awareness and taking responsibility cost us nothing and could very well save our lives.

At some point we will be called on to support a close friend or family member who is ill. This requires stoicism from us, a strength to be there unconditionally for them, however tough we may find it. Nursing someone raises all sorts of issues for us, forcing us to question our own fragility and mortality. Talk these feelings through with your loved ones, never with those you are supporting. They shouldn't feel the need to support and reassure *you*, whilst facing their own crisis. Instead, ask them how they can best be supported by you. Many people are terrified, not knowing what to say when someone is sick. Don't avoid the sick – tell them you don't know what to say. Being ill, or nursing someone who is ill, can often make us more honest, confident, and outspoken. We let people know that what they are saying is helpful or otherwise and we only surround ourselves with those who support us and make us feel more able to cope. Make sure you are one of these people, someone who radiates support and love.

Fitness and nutrition in midlife

In my life before children, being fit was important, much of my social life revolved around sport. As a student I exercised almost everyday: squash, yoga, tennis, cycling, circuit training were the usual combination. When the children were growing up, I stopped finding the time for sport apart from yoga, which was my saviour. Yoga turned into Pilates and during my divorce I learned kick-boxing. During emotionally painful days I walked the poor dog's legs off. And I missed sport. I missed the 'high' I got when I was fit, I missed and longed for the extra energy I had. Yes, I walked and always took the stairs rather than the lift, but it just wasn't enough. Fitness and keeping in shape is vital in midlife. It's tough, that is indeed a fact. We recover more slowly and it takes us longer in the gym or at our favoured sport. Also, we lose the results quickly if we take time off. Feeling fit is something I now could not do without. It is firmly back in my daily routine.

What are the essentials for a fitter midlife?

A regular cardio workout is to be encouraged and no expensive gym membership is required, so no excuses! We can walk, cycle, swim, take the stairs (always), park further away from the office or get off one stop before our usual one. Just get the heart beating a little faster.

Muscle strength is vital too. There are plenty of YouTube videos or apps for your smartphone which you can watch and follow for firming up those parts of us that need a little more attention now we're in midlife – arms, abs, legs and bums in particular.

I do some exercise every day. This is my routine: I do

The Plank, an incredible all-round exercise for one minute. This engages a whole load of muscles the entire length of our body in order to hold this position. It hurts like hell, so be warned! Is it worth it? Absolutely yes. Look it up online, commit to doing it every day and notice the difference. Begin with ten seconds and build up to one minute. I also follow an Abs App on my phone for approximately ten minutes of varied exercises. Press-ups, for me, are a killer, but I am committed to slowly building up and will not let them beat me. A girlfriend told me she does fifty . . . I can barely do five without collapsing in tears . . . yet.

Deciding to exercise is a hard undertaking, but one that I work into my day because I know how much better, emotionally and physically, I feel for doing it.

Nutrition is another major commitment for me. It is very true that we are what we eat. I know how good I feel when my diet is filled with fresh fruit and vegetables, herbs, nuts and seeds. I also know how sluggish and tired I feel when it is filled with sugar, processed food and too much alcohol. It's not rocket science. But I'm no saint and don't deny myself the things I love – cheese, coffee, chocolate, and a decent glass of wine being the four main ones. My one proviso is that they have to be excellent – everything in moderation, my grandmother used to say.

My diet does include a range of superfoods. I've read much and urge you to do the same and decide what you can easily add to your diet to help with a whole raft of health issues that face us in midlife. If you are able, I think it's worth having a consultation with a nutritionist who specialises in midlife too. With most superfoods, the clinical research is limited and most evidence is anecdotal, so you're either a believer in foods supporting our health or not. I am, but it's up to you to decide for yourself.

I include the following in my daily food intake:

- **Apple cider vinegar** (raw and unfiltered only) has been known to help with allergies, balancing the acids in our body, detoxing, aiding weight loss, sinus infections, colds, sore throats, candida, acne and dermatitis and easing joint pain. I take one teaspoon in a small glass of water first thing in the morning . . . Believe me, you get used to it.

- **Chia seeds** are amazing little seeds that are high in Omega 3 and 6 and soluble fibre. Known as Indian Running Food for their sustained energy giving. They are high in antioxidants and rich in protein, calcium and potassium. If you have a sluggish gut then make sure you include them in your diet. I love them and add them to my breakfast.

- **Aloe vera juice** tastes like it's good for you! It's amazing and I've drunk it every day for over ten years. It is said to aid digestion, promote healthy skin, detoxes, has powerful anti-inflammatory properties and is full of vitamins, minerals and amino acids.

- **Maca** is another superfood which is believed to boost sexual function, help with menopause symptoms, improve energy and balance mood.

- **Flaxseed** (also known as linseed) is extremely high in Omega 3, which helps lower cholesterol, is anti-inflammatory, keeps our brains functioning well and improves skin health.

- **Hemp** contains all nine of the essential amino acids our bodies need, high amounts of fatty acids and fibre, and is a great source of vegetarian protein.

- **Almonds** support brain function (hurrah) and they also lower cholesterol and help build strong bones and teeth.

- **Turmeric** is often referred to as the Queen of Spices. It contains a wide range of antioxidant, anti-viral, anti-bacterial, anti-fungal, anti-carcinogenic, and anti-inflammatory properties. Amazing stuff! Add it to your salad dressings or your cereal every day.

- **Ginger** supports digestion, i.e., relieves stomach cramps and gas, is anti-fungal and antibiotic, relieves nausea and car sickness. Oh, and it's a great aphrodisiac too.

I make my own granola for breakfast and snacking, it takes ten minutes to prepare and an hour or so in the oven (recipe on page 148). I juice most mornings too (see page 150) because it's a brilliant way to get a ton of raw vegetables and fruit into your system first thing in the morning. And the children love them too . . . well, maybe not the green ones so much.

Menopause

Is it the menopause that truly marks our transition into midlife? All of us females will go through the menopause, the ultimate 'change' in life. How we cope with it is individual. But how do we approach the menopause? Do we see it as the beginning of the end for us or are we doing a 'yippee, no more periods' dance?

Some women sail through their menopause, barely noticing it, whilst others suffer each and every symptom. Much has been written about this change in life and I'm not here to add to the thousands of words that have been written in books, articles and online. My approach is to question our attitude to this natural phenomenon and how we choose to react to it.

For those of us who have struggled with fertility, it does mark the end of our hopes of conceiving a child and this can cause psychological problems that must be addressed if we are to accept our menopause without cursing and raging with each symptom.

Do we have a choice about how we go through our menopause? We cannot know in advance what symptoms we'll get or how long the process will last; however, in the twenty-first century there is surely no need to 'suffer' through our menopause. There are enough pharmaceutical and natural products on the market to ease our way through the symptoms.

- Be proactive, read all you can about it.
- Yes, you'll sweat at night like you have the flu, so be prepared with fresh sheets, towels and T-shirts before going to bed.
- Retain your sense of humour throughout.
- Acknowledge it without letting it rule your life.
- Find out about solutions for your symptoms rather than focusing on the problems.
- Eat well and look out for natural remedies.
- Accepting it as part of life goes a long way to easing the passage through it.
- It *will* come to an end.
- Don't use it as a means to complain about life.

Family life and changing roles

Those of us blessed with having parents and in-laws who are still relatively fit and well will have begun, nevertheless, to have concerns. We worry about any forgetfulness of theirs and fear it is the start of something more serious. We worry about their aching joints. We worry about their peers becoming ill and how that affects them psychologically. We worry about them coping in such a technological world. We begin to find our roles reversing and this needs to be handled with care because we often find ourselves parenting our own parents. This we need to prepare ourselves for. Patience is something that we would do well to master at this stage. We forget that we are no longer the small children and they the all-knowing parent. Now might be a good time to confront and deal with any residual issues we might have with our parents. Often the critical, short-tempered, tough parent we remember as a child now needs our love, patience and understanding as they age.

Some of our parents are determined to live a full life and go off on any number of adventures, totally embracing their lives. Others, sadly, fall into a 'learned helplessness' role and this can be extraordinarily challenging. Some are plagued with physical illness and we must find a way to support them without disempowering them too.

We women in midlife are frequently referred to as the 'sandwich generation' as we care for elderly parents whilst our children are still at home. And as we live longer, and our children often remain at home longer, this can put an enormous strain on both us and those around us. It is not uncommon to sit at the hub of four generations – parents and in-laws, ourselves, our children and grandchildren. One friend is dealing with her sick and ageing father who lives three hours away and cares for her elderly mother-in-law whilst, at the same time, preparing her daughter for secondary school.

I'm not sure what the solution is. I suspect we must acknowledge that we can't be all things to all people if we are to remain sane. I also know that this is when we call on our women friends, our tribe, who support us through all things and without whom we wouldn't be as resilient as we are.

New careers and becoming a student

There's change afoot. Some of us are returning to work, some of us are going back to studying, some are setting up our own businesses. All of this is challenging as it requires courage and faith in ourselves and this often comes at a time when we are questioning our abilities.

I have friends leaving senior corporate roles for a complete change and heading off to study once more. I have friends retraining and going back to work having taken many years off to raise their families. I have friends who find themselves becoming the sole breadwinners as their marriages have ended and they need to become financially independent quickly. I have friends who are leaving employment to become their own boss.

It's a risk many of us are taking. It requires a leap of faith. We need to find a way to live through the chaos of not knowing, of being in freefall for a time whilst we find a balance once more. One friend said she went through a mourning period for the career and woman she was before deciding to accept redundancy in order to fulfil her dream of completely changing direction and heading back to study. She has had to come to terms with the change in income, learning that the skills she had built in her career aren't necessarily the same ones she'll need from now on. She has to unlearn, in order to relearn. She questions herself on the 'madness' of her decision to 'throw it all away' and then remembers exactly why she's choosing to follow her dream.

Stepping out into the great unknown, whether returning to work for the first time in decades or leaving employment to study or set up on our own, is both terrifying and exciting. There is no template. We must get used to letting go, of not knowing the answers, and this is where great creativity comes from. Remind yourself of your brave decision. Acknowledge your courage. Would you wish life to be easy and straightforward? Surely it wouldn't be worth doing if it weren't challenging?

Whatever the skills we have gathered over the decades, we will carry them forward in some shape or form. Women returning to the workplace after years caring for children can feel inadequate and unable to compete in the workplace, but we must acknowledge the importance of these so-called 'soft' skills and have faith in our abilities.

If we are making career changes, we may find we need to help our family adjust, and that can be challenging and need careful management We may need to train them to do more, to accept that we're not always there.

Travelling solo

For those of us with children who have spent many hours of our parenting lives organising passports and travel documents, packing suitcases and standing in check-ins whilst keeping an eye on children who either suddenly need the loo or are hungry/thirsty/tired/moody/overexcited, the sheer joy of packing one bag and making ones' own way to the airport, browsing the shops, enjoying a coffee/glass of something is nothing short of sublime.

It can feel such a strange experience, so used are we to having children and/or partner with us that, to begin with, we keep wondering what we've forgotten. A number of times, I had that sinking feeling that I'd left something behind. My solo travelling has only gone as far as visiting friends overseas – I have as yet not spent time alone in another city or holiday destination – and I asked friends for their experiences of travelling alone as a woman in midlife and it was all positive.

- To spend time in solitude and to travel within myself is to be greatly encouraged.
- To do as I wish without needing to take anyone else into consideration.
- To be without schedule, to eat and sleep when I want to.
- To be utterly focused on my needs and desires.
- To truly 'marvel' at my surroundings.
- To spend time in complete silence enabling me to 'listen' more.
- To sit and watch the world go by without having to converse with anyone.

One friend summed up her solo travelling this way, 'It did not feel a bit like loneliness. It felt like an invitation to a feast.' I like that.

Our greatest fears and turning them around

We can look at our future in midlife in two ways. We can fear it or we can embrace it – no surprise where I sit!

That is not to say that I'm some mad, delusional, positive-thinking hippy with no foothold in reality. Life happens. However, as you know by now, it is up to us how we deal with it. I know many who live in fear: fear of ageing, fear of dying, fear of being alone, fear of losing their validity at work, fear of the children leaving home, fear of their partner finding a younger version, fear of illness . . . If we are not careful we become so consumed by our fears that we end up fearing life itself.

Do the practical stuff to put your mind at rest. Is your will up to date? Who has power of attorney? Do you have a funeral plan? Speak to your children (with humour) about your plans and arrangements. Knowing that all this is arranged will bring comfort to you and your family. Now . . . go live your life.

I remember an exercise I did years back on a course I attended. We spent time in thought imagining we were old and in our final days. What were our thoughts about our life? What did we wish we had done more of? What did we wish we had done less of? It was an enlightening and, at the same time, sobering exercise.

- Should our fear of getting older prevent us from living our life today?
- Should our fear of cancer prevent us from living a full and healthy life today?

- Should our fear of our children leaving home stop us from enjoying our time with them today?
- Should our fear of losing out on a promotion because we're older prevent us from giving it our all today?
- Should our fear of having sex with a new partner after the ending of a long marriage prevent us from embarking on a potentially fulfilling relationship?

Odes to midlife

I emailed a group of friends to ask them their thoughts on midlife, how it was affecting them and what their fears and hopes were. Some of their replies have been incorporated into the text above, but there were some that particularly stood out for me and, with their permission, I include them here.

'After we talked today I was thinking about your book and realised I didn't respond to your message asking for thoughts on midlife. Ironically, this appears to be one of my many problems – sometimes I think I've actually done something, when all I've done is think about it. Senior moments? Here (in brief) are some things: dealing with my husband's midlife crisis – could write a book on that alone! Parents a long way away – what do we do when they need more help? How did I end up being financially dependent

on my husband? All the decisions seemed right at the time
. . . yet here I am, earning less than I did when I was
twenty-five. To Botox or not to Botox . . . just want to look
in a mirror and not look tired/cross. Knee pain/period
pain/stomach pain/skin problems – I challenge any doctor
to diagnose any ailment in a forty-five plus woman without
using the word 'menopause'! Alcohol tolerance level seems
to be getting lower and lower . . . How the hell have I got
cellulite on my arms? Knowing all the right things to eat
but never following through. However, my vanity always
outweighs the aversion to exercise when my comfy trousers
become 'uncomfy'. I used to love clothes shopping – it was
all about showing off – now it's all about covering up. So,
although most of these points may seem frivolous, some are
serious.'

AB

•

'I've hit a wall with work and am coming to the realisation
that I am probably too old to retrain once again – it's a
scary thought. Does this mean that this might therefore be
'it'? I'm hacked off with earning barely a thing; wishing
I really did have a professional qualification that entitled
me to proper work and a proper income (not for the first
time wishing I really had continued with law school, even
though, deep down, I know I'd have hated it).

Feel very weird about having one of the children here part time, who's also confused about his role, i.e., wanting to be the child, (where everything is done for him), behaving like a stroppy teenager, but actually being an adult. The realisation that maybe we can't all live together any more, that we have outgrown each other. Excited and frightened about what this means as 'the next stage' looms. Not sure if I'm sad or happy at not being needed as a mother in quite the same way as I was . . .

Don't enjoy looking in mirror and seeing more lines, yes I know, I laugh too much . . . ageing skin is not a fun issue, and also as I NEVER put my face in the sun, why do I have wrinkles anyway? Facial hair, whose idea was that?

Really not relishing the fact of ageing parents and all that entails. Dealing with the mother-in-law again who seems to revert, every so often, to the original cantankerous version.

Hate how negative I sound . . . having never been depressed, I find it difficult to deal with as I know it's all about my own self-worth which I always attach to me working . . . and then we are back to point one above . . .

On a positive note, absolutely love the open and loving relationships I have with the children, who are gorgeous, happy, bright and independent and who CHOOSE to be with us. Looking forward to spending lots of time alone with the beloved, as it's why I married him in the first place.

Oh and one last thing . . . I only want to shop in Topshop but know I'd look ridiculous! Ho hum . . .'

SP

•

'*Ageing parents* – making the choice of how to balance my life with their increasing needs. The emotional and practical impacts and insights.

Hair colour – yes or no? Like the idea of ageing naturally, and saving hairdresser costs. Also, damn it, there are more white hairs appearing!

Dating – Yes, right. At this rate I will be meeting Mr Right in my sixties. Too long not dating, now fear there will be expectation of familiarity with the whole being in a relationship thing. Basically being a woose, still.

*Caree*r – Yes. Mine is not sustainable yet. I've made the move towards what I love, now it's the profitability bit. Feels odd to be starting again at this age – but actually I have heard of many starting businesses in their seventies and eighties. So. Carry on.

Fitness and Diet – I know what works for me. I've learned that gentle exercise is what I prefer. No more gym beastings. Perhaps because I exercise more for my own benefit, not punitive stress release. And diet – I know what I prefer.

I know to ignore magazines that claim to know what is good and not good. I listen more to my own body's signals.

Financial Independence – Oh so yes. But because self-employed, that is now also really just independence. It's like a second growing up, realising that parents will not always be there to bail me out #GetAGrip. Also, getting organised with wills, insurance, investments . . . all that stuff.

Spirituality – feeling free to express this in whatever way I choose. For me that means it is important to connect with others, and I don't give a monkeys about formal religion.

Letting go – friends, family, secure job . . . things that used to be part of the routine aren't or won't always be there. Realising nothing lasts, whether I love it or don't like it (partly enhanced by observing how many of my parents' pals and siblings are dying out).

Healing – my family is coming back together after years apart. More open expression of affection. More conversations about who we are and what we like. More acceptance. More love.'

    KJ

•

'Midlife . . . funny isn't it, one daughter told me once
that I wasn't old I was middle-aged, and the other one
completely got that that was worse than being old . . . So
what does fifty mean to me? I thought I would be talking
about negatives – the fact that it is hard to get a job at this
age if you have hopped off the career ladder for a few
years, the dodgy memory, being the sandwich generation
still with the feeling of not giving enough time to everyone including myself, the weight gain (oh hello, where did
that come from?) but it's not that which springs to mind
althoughthey do loom large and maybe I have been really
lucky with the menopause in that it passed by without too
much fuss.

I find that I have a quiet confidence that I never had before,
that I can make the choice to live on my own happily, go
on holiday on my own, wear what I want, sit in a café or
pub (though not yet in a restaurant in the evening), on my
own if I choose, can sit in with a book on a Saturday night
and not feel I'm missing out but feel content that I can stay
in. I am happy that my children are moving on, loving the
fact that I am healthy, can run regularly, go to the gym and
I don't feel the need to compete on any level with anyone.
Women complain that at this age they disappear – and it is
a little sobering sometimes not to be noticed – but it's also
quite relaxing to enjoy just being without needing to be
on show, to feel the need to attract attention, to worry that

everything is perfect. But then again, if I want to be noticed I can still rock the heels and lipstick if I choose to – wear the purple hat – because like most women today I have the choice. Like no women before us, we have more choice, which can be overwhelming unless we choose not to be overwhelmed but empowered.'

MP

•

'*Taking the plunge* – The pain of starting again on a new career path – and I mean "pain". Having had a career, downsized it for children and then procrastinating about wanting to do something different (for several years). Putting my toe in the water by way of an evening course and then taking the plunge and becoming a student again. At first feeling completely incompetent and starting at the bottom . . . until the realisation that, instead of mourning the loss of those years of experience, I can build on them with the new skills I'm learning. Financially I'm now dependent on my husband and that's been a huge adjustment for both of us. I'm constantly feeling guilt about not earning and using the words 'retraining' when anyone asks.

The Sandwich – My daughter is growing up fast but still very much needs me as a mum and then on the other side are ageing parents for whom at times you become the

grown-up. Illness, hospital visits, being a carer and dealing with the care system, setting up powers of attorney
and sorting finances. At the same time the grieving process
starts as you feel you are losing them day by day. It makes
you think about your own mortality and in my case reminding myself to appreciate what I have.

The Changeling – Where did that muffin top come from?
And trying to get rid of it is almost impossible. I feel more
comfortable in my own skin and with myself, but don't
look too often in the mirror as then I start to contemplate
surgery. My friends and I laugh about our night sweats and
hot flushes but the acceptance of what this really means is
a hard adjustment.'

CR

How do we define success in midlife?
What makes the ultimate midlife woman?

I'd put money on it not being about the things we surround
ourselves with, the size of our home, the money we have
stashed in the bank, the letters we have after our name, the
name on the office door or the car we drive. Success for us
women is something much more powerful, deeper and res-
onant. Success for me is illustrated in the fifty life lessons
and in these points opposite:

- Courage to make decisions for her life.
- Standing up for what she believe in.
- Passion for her life, for her work, for those she loves.
- Vulnerability which shows her as human and not some comic strip super-heroine.
- Gentleness and compassion.
- Her tribe of girlfriends.
- Knowing that happiness and fulfilment is an inside job.
- Responsibility for herself.
- Acceptance of herself and the circumstances of her life.
- Self-confidence and inner beauty, an irresistibly sexy combination.
- Knowing that it's never too late to do something new.
- Embracing and sitting at ease with her imperfections.
- A fulfilling career or cause she is passionate about.
- Happy children that have roots and wings.
- Having a meaningful life.
- Being part of and contributing to the wider community.
- Teaching her sons to respect all women.
- Teaching her daughters to value themselves as women.
- Being proud of her own achievements in balancing a home life and career.
- Making a difference in people's lives.

Midlife reminds me of childbirth and motherhood. We don't really know how it's going to turn out. There are books we can read and advice we can get from those that care for us but we have to go through it ourselves to experience it. I made childbirth up as I went along because my carefully written birth plan never made it out of my overnight bag. Thank goodness I was flexible enough in my thinking to allow the midwives to do their jobs. Motherhood was pretty much the same. I fed on demand, loved and held and kissed my babies. I dismissed the advice that I was 'spoiling' them. I was setting them up for life by teaching them about love.

Midlife feels a bit the same. It's time to rip up the 'old wisdom' book that states we're over the hill and it's full speed all the way to old age. Stuff that, I say. This is a rebirth. This is where we finally get to create our life our way for all the reasons I've given in the Fifty Lessons. I don't remember who said it or when I heard it, but these words echo around in my head when I consider my own midlife, 'How shall we live? How shall we be?'

Let's not wait for something catastrophic to happen in our life to make changes. Eat well and exercise *now* rather than wait until the doctor tells us that we need to sort ourselves out. Communicate *now* with our partner rather than bearing grudges and feeling resentment. Ask for what we want in our relationships *now*. Work on ourselves *now:* it is, after all, the most important and valuable relationship we will ever have.

I am optimistic that we can live the second half of our lives with purpose, with hope for new beginnings for many of us. Whether that be in love, in a new career, in a home without our children. Do not let the past define who we are today and who we can be tomorrow. Without doubt, the past has helped create the women we are, but we can choose to redefine ourselves for a different tomorrow.

Friends, let us take our inspiration from the late, great Nora Ephron, 'Be the heroine of your life, not the victim.'

Who's with me?

Listen, Read, Cook

Kitchen disco playlist
. . . a selection

'Move On Up' by Curtis Mayfield

'Smooth' by Santana, featuring Rob Thomas

'Respect' by Aretha Franklin

'I Need a Dollar' by Aloe Blacc

'Ride on Time' by Black Box

'Pump It' by The Black Eyed Peas

'Good Times' by Chic

'Jammin'' by Bob Marley

'Single Ladies' by Beyoncé

'Sir Duke' by Stevie Wonder

'Let's Groove' by Earth, Wind and Fire

'Funky Town' by Lipps Inc.

'Show Me Love' by Robin S.

'Celebration' by Kool and the Gang

'Somebody Else's Guy' by Jocelyn Brown

'I'm Coming Out' by Diana Ross

'Sex Machine' by James Brown

'Theme from Shaft' by Isaac Hayes

'Billie Jean' by Michael Jackson

'Cuba' by Gibson Brothers

'I Will Survive' by Gloria Gaynor

'I Feel Love' by Donna Summer

'She Drive Me Crazy' by Fine Young Cannibals

'Stayin' Alive' by Bee Gees

'What a Feeling' by Irene Cara

'You're The One For Me' by D-Train

'I'm Every Woman' by Chaka Khan

'I'm Too Sexy' by Right Said Fred

'Boogie Wonderland' by Earth, Wind and Fire

'Hot Stuff' by Donna Summer

'U Can't Touch This' by MC Hammer

'Groove is in the Hall' by Deee-Lite

'Finally' by CeCe Peniston

'Ladies Night' by Kool and the Gang

'Don't Stop The Music' by Yarborough & Peoples

'I Just Want to Make Love to You' by Etta James

'Crazy' by Gnarls Barkley

'Never Gonna Give You Up' by Rick Astley

'Boogie Nights' by Heatwave

'Play That Funky Music' by Wild Cherry

'Love on Top' by Beyoncé

'Shame' by Evelyn 'Champagne' King

'Grace Kelly' by Mika

'Beggin'' by Madcon

'I Am What I Am' by Gloria Gaynor

'I'm So Excited' by The Pointer Sisters

My bookshelf

Some of the books that have inspired me and those I turn to when I'm stuck.

The Four Agreements: Practical Guide to Personal Wisdom (Toltec Wisdom) by Don Miguel Ruiz

Broken Open: How difficult times can help us grow by Elizabeth Lesser

Daring Greatly: How the Courage to Be Vulnerable Transforms the Way We Live, Love, Parent, and Lead by Brené Brown

Eat, Pray, Love: One Woman's Search for Everything by Elizabeth Gilbert

You Can Heal Your Life by Louise Hay

Simple Abundance: A Daybook of Comfort and Joy by Sarah Ban Breathnach

Walking in This World: Spiritual strategies for forging your creative trail by Julia Cameron

Dear Lover by David Deida

Jonathan Livingston Seagull: A Story by Richard Bach

The Alchemist by Paulo Coelho

A Return to Love: Reflections on the Principles of a 'Course in Miracles' by Marianne Williamson

Pride and Prejudice by Jane Austen

10 Secrets for Success and Inner Peace by Dr Wayne Dyer

The Monk Who Sold His Ferrari by Robin S Sharma

The Poetry of Mary Oliver

My recipes

Granola

This is all about experimenting; there are no hard and fast rules. I use whatever I have in the house so make it up as you go along. Cook depending on how crunchy you like your granola. I have adapted this recipe from the original in Bill Collison's cookbook *Cook, Eat, Smile*.

- 700g jumbo oats (must be jumbo – regular make it more like flapjacks)
- 175g nuts (whatever you have in the house – I love almonds)
- 50g seeds (pumpkin, sesame, sunflower). I add chia, linseed and hemp when I'm eating it
- half a teaspoon of ground cinnamon
- a good grating of fresh whole nutmeg
- 100ml flavourless oil (I use sunflower)
- 50ml water
- 200g of something sweet (I use a combination of honey, muscovado sugar, golden syrup, agave – it all depends what I've got in the house.) Add more or less according to your taste
- 2 tsp vanilla extract.

Preheat oven to 140°C/120°C fan/gas 1

Heat the oil, water, sweeteners and vanilla extract until melted. I do this in the microwave, it can equally be done over a low heat on the stove. Stir to combine. Pour over the dry ingredients and mix well. Line a large baking tray with baking parchment. Tip the oat mixture onto the tray and spread out. Put into the oven for 45 minutes. Take out and stir, lower oven temperature to 120°C/100°C fan/gas 1/2 and cook for another 30 to 40 minutes. Take out to cool.

Keep in an airtight box – it won't last long. This will make approximately 14 servings.

I serve with a few spoonfuls of chia, linseed and hemp seeds along with whatever fresh and dried fruit I have in the fridge or cupboard, plus a few dollops of yoghurt.

Juicing

I love my juicer, and no, it's no real trouble to clean it out afterwards. I didn't spend a fortune on it, either!

I have found that by trial and error it's easy to come up with tasty combinations. Don't be afraid to try what appeals to you. Wash the fruit and vegetables before using, no need to peel them – the machine deals with that. The following combinations will make a couple of glasses full. Cheers!

Green Juice
— 2 to 3 apples, half a cucumber, 2 sticks of celery, half an inch of root ginger (or more if you like it a little spicy), a couple of slices of lemon, a good handful of kale and/or spinach leaves

Orange Juice
— 2 to 3 apples, 4 to 5 carrots, a couple of slices of lemon, half an inch of root ginger — again more if you like it spicy

Purple Juice
— 2 to 3 apples, 4 carrots, half a peeled cucumber, 1 stick of celery, half a raw beetroot (absolutely NOT the cooked beetroot in vinegar!)

Girls' Night In Food

Here are some recipes that I've used for my Girls' Nights In. They are all simple, easy-to-make dishes for your own Girls' Night In using fresh or store-cupboard ingredients to put together recipes with big, blousy flavours. The fine dining of *Masterchef* it isn't!

Prawn Thai curry with mango

Adapted from a Nigella special. Serves 4

- 300g raw prawns
- 1 medium butternut squash
- 1 tablespoon of red Thai curry paste, ready-made or make your own – add more or less according to your taste
- 1 tablespoon olive oil
- 1 teaspoon sesame seed oil
- 200g green beans/pak choi/mushrooms/spinach – use whichever you have to hand, there is no limit
- 400ml coconut milk
- A handul of fresh coriander leaves, chopped
- 1 mango, cubed

Marinade some big raw prawns in bought red Thai curry paste or make up your own with an inch of ginger, one chopped red chilli, a clove of garlic, a handful of coriander, half a stick of lemongrass, a heaped teaspoon of cumin seeds and the zest and juice of one lime all blitzed together.

Roast a diced butternut squash until it's started to take on some colour and has begun to soften. In a large, non-stick wok heat some olive oil and a teaspoon or two of roasted sesame oil, add the squash and whatever other vegetables you're using – green beans, mushrooms. Put the lid on to steam for a few minutes. Add the coconut milk or cream depending on what you have to hand. When it's bubbling, add the raw prawns and stir through the diced mango right at the end. Just before serving add plenty of chopped coriander.

Chicken with sundried tomatoes, tarragon and paprika

An old family favourite, adapted from the original by Josceline Dimbleby

- 4 chicken breasts
- juice of 1 lemon
- 2 tsp paprika (sweet or hot depending on your preference)
- 1 tbsp fresh tarragon, chopped
- 1 clove garlic, crushed
- 1 tbsp olive oil
- 6 sun-dried tomatoes, sliced
- 200ml crème fraiche, low-fat
- salt and pepper, to taste
- half a teaspoon of chilli powder, to taste (optional)

Slice chicken breasts finely, place in a dish (large enough to allow the chicken to be in one layer) with the lemon juice, paprika, tarragon and garlic (and chilli if using). Leave to marinade for as long as you've got (at least an hour). Pour the olive oil into a heavy frying pan and place on a medium heat; add the chicken mixture and cook fairly gently for 10 minutes until the chicken is cooked through. During this time add the sliced sun-dried tomatoes. Transfer the chicken to a plate and keep warm. Turn up the heat and add the crème fraiche and allow to bubble away for a few minutes. Taste, then season with salt and pepper if it needs it. Put the chicken back into the pan and mix well. Pour out onto a platter and either cover with foil and keep warm until needed or serve straight away.

This will serve 4 easily and can easily be doubled to serve more as part of a buffet.

Mixed salad with ciabatta and toasted seeds

I love great big salad bowls filled with all sorts of leaves and toasted seeds mixed with diced cucumber and avocado and chunky, oven-baked ciabatta croutons and a whole pile of fresh herbs. There are no rules – just do your own thing!

Quinoa lentil salad with roasted tomatoes and pan-fried red peppers

This is a lovely colourful salad and is so very good for you.
Serves 6

- 350g small vine tomatoes/cherry tomatoes
- 3 tbsp extra virgin olive oil
- sprigs of thyme
- salt and pepper, to taste
- 200g quinoa
- 100g lentils (basic green ones or snazzy Puy ones)
- 2 red peppers, sliced
- handful fresh herbs, chopped

Halve the tomatoes and place on a lined baking sheet. Drizzle over one tablespoon of the olive oil, season and add a few sprigs of thyme. Cook in a low oven for an hour or so – what you're looking for is the concentrated flavours of semi-dried tomatoes (you could of course pay for these at the deli counter but your own are so easy to make and taste much better).

Cook the quinoa and lentils according to the packet instructions. Transfer both to a large bowl and pour over one tablespoon of olive oil to stop it all sticking together. Leave to cool.

Slice up the red peppers and fry with the reamaining oil in a big pan over a high heat. You want them cooked through but with a bit of charring around the edges. (If you don't like the skin then you can grill half peppers until they are blackened, stick them in a sealed plastic bag to sweat the skins off and then slice them.) When everything is cooked and cooled, gently mix together and add a dressing of your choice, then sprinkle with the herbs.

Couscous, roasted vegetables, chorizo and halloumi

Serves 6

- 300g couscous
- 360 ml stock, homemade or a good-quality vegetable stock cube
- 100g chorizo, diced
- approximately 500g of your favourite vegetables – red peppers, onions, courgettes, aubergines, squash, carrots in proportions to your taste – there is no right or wrong here!
- 1 tsp chilli powder – according to taste
- 2 tbsp olive oil
- 250g halloumi, sliced
- a big handful of fresh herbs (e.g. parsley, chives, thyme, mint) chopped
- baby salad leaves

Pour the boiling hot stock over the couscous and cover until absorbed. Using a fork, separate the grains to make it light and fluffy. Roast the vegetables in the olive oil and chilli (if you fancy it) in a hot oven for about 30–40 mins. Whilst they are roasting, fry the chorizo until the oil runs and it's beginning to get nice and crispy. Remove from the heat and drain on some kitchen paper. Add some sliced halloumi to the pan and fry for a few minutes on each side until golden. In a large serving dish/platter pile up the layers – couscous on the bottom followed by the roasted vegetables, then the chorizo with the halloumi on top. Scatter the herbs and surround with the baby salad leaves. Serve with a dressing of your choice.

You can make a dressing with lots of olive oil, lime juice, ground cumin and chilli or cayenne pepper. (I dry-fry cumin seeds until they become fragrant. Once they've cooled, put them in a pestle and mortar and pound until they become powder (don't worry about it looking like the shop-bought ground cumin – this stuff tastes so much nicer – and you can buy big bags from the international aisle in the supermarket).

Chocolate brownies with raspberries

Use your favourite brownie recipe, the one that always works for you and your oven, but before pouring the batter into the lined tin add a couple of handfuls of fresh or frozen and defrosted raspberries (I've also used blackberries – delicious) and stir through. Pour the mixture into your tin and bake until the top has just set and is cracking at the sides of the tin. Remember that brownies need to be squidgy-looking as they come out of the oven, otherwise you'll end up with chocolate cake instead.

Seasonal fruit/compote

I love fruit and always have a bowl of fruit piled on the table and sometimes will make a compote.

Spring – slice up some sticks of rhubarb with a grating of fresh ginger or some sliced blood oranges and a little sugar or honey to sweeten. Cook gently in a medium oven for 30 minutes. Delicious warm or cold.

Summer – no need to cook, just pile strawberries, raspberries, melon, peaches, blueberries or whatever else you find in the market or supermarket into a pretty dish.

Autumn – plums, blackberries, apples and pears cooked in their own juices. You can always add some sugar to taste if it's too sharp for you.

Winter – it's all dried fruit – apricots, prunes, figs, apple rings – put into a pan and cook gently with some fruit juice and a dash of something alcoholic if you fancy.

More from Rebecca Perkins

If you've enjoyed this book and would like to find out more then head over to my website www.rebperkins.com. There you'll find blogs to inspire you, a free audio, seven top tips when you sign up for to my mailing list and a growing community of like-minded women journeying through midlife. You can jump straight in and book a one-to-one Skype call with me or take it slower and sign up for one of my online courses.

I can also be found having conversations on . . .

Facebook: www.facebook.com/BestKnickersAlways

Twitter: @rebperkins1

Instagram: www.instagram.com/beabodacious

Pinterest: www.pinterest.com/beabodacious

Notes

Today I am grateful for . . .

....

....

....

....

....

....

....

....

....

....

....

....

In my life I want less . . .

....

....

....

....

....

....

....

....

....

....

....

....

In my life I want more . . .

. . . .

. . . .

. . . .

. . . .

. . . .

. . . .

. . . .

. . . .

. . . .

. . . .

. . . .

. . . .

How does the next chapter of my life begin?

....

....

....

....

....

....

....

....

....

....

....

....